CASSEROLES

GOOD
HOUSEKEEPING

CASSEROLES

60 FABULOUS ONE-DISH RECIPES

★ GOOD FOOD GUARANTEED ★

HEARST
books

HEARSTBOOKS

An Imprint of Sterling Publishing
1166 Avenue of the Americas
New York, NY 10036

ISBN 978-1-61837-202-4

GOOD HOUSEKEEPING

Jane Francisco
EDITOR IN CHIEF
Melissa Geurts
DESIGN DIRECTOR
Susan Westmoreland
FOOD DIRECTOR
Sharon Franke
FOOD APPLIANCES DIRECTOR

Cover Design: Scott Russo
Interior Design: Barbara Balch
Project Editor: Carol Prager

The Good Housekeeping Cookbook Seal guarantees that the recipes in this cookbook meet the strict standards
of the Good Housekeeping Research Institute. The Institute has been a source of reliable information and a
consumer advocate since 1900, and established its seal of approval in 1909. Every recipe has been triple-tested
for ease, reliability, and great taste.

www.goodhousekeeping.com

For information about custom editions, special sales, and premium and corporate purchases, please contact
Sterling Special Sales at 800-805-5489 or specialsales@sterlingpublishing.com.

Distributed in Canada by Sterling Publishing
c/o Canadian Manda Group, 664 Annette Street
Toronto, Ontario, Canada M6S 2C8
Distributed in Australia by Capricorn Link (Australia) Pty. Ltd.
P.O. Box 704, Windsor, NSW 2756, Australia

Manufactured in China

2 4 6 8 10 9 7 5 3 1

www.sterlingpublishing.com

CONTENTS

Creole "Cassoulet"
(page 95)

Foreword

Do you remember your first casserole? I was convinced I'd never eaten one until my college roommate introduced me to her mother's chicken and rice dish. But I was wrong. Though my family's repertoire didn't include classics like King Ranch, Tuna Noodle, or Green Bean, it turns out I'd been feasting on casseroles like Lasagna, Eggplant Parmigiana, and Manicotti since I was able to sit up. My family believed in starting solid food early!

By definition, casseroles are all about the dish. If you cook the food or even finish it off in a baking dish, it's a casserole. Now do you remember your first casserole? It's the perfect food, whether you're making dinner for your family, feeding a crowd, schlepping a dish to a potluck, or even making dessert. Casseroles are a satisfying—and easy—way to go.

In this volume, we've collected over 60 of our all-time favorites, so you're sure to find an easy and irresistible one-dish dinner, or breakfast, to tempt you any day of the week. We start with the basics: ingredients, equipment, prep shortcuts, do-ahead options, and freezing (and reheating) instructions. Then it's on to the order of the day. For breakfast, check out our cheesy grits casserole and several riffs on stratas and overnight French toast. Family dinner? We haven't left out classics like Shepherd's Pie, Mac 'n' Cheese, Lasagna, or Tuna-Melt, but you'll also find yummy updates like Creamy Chicken & Mushroom Pie, Baked Pasta e Fagioli, and Greek Ziti Bake. Entertaining? Italian Wedding Pasta, Louisiana Seafood Casserole, and Creole "Cassoulet" are all party perfect. Dessert? I'm trying to decide between Deep-Dish Apple Cobbler and Spiced Chocolate Bread Pudding.

In the Good Housekeeping Test Kitchens, our team develops, triple-tests, and, yes, tastes every recipe that carries our name. For this book we tested to make sure recipes work in any oven, with any brand of ingredients, no matter what . . . So what are you waiting for? Delicious, one-dish dinners await.

SUSAN WESTMORELAND
Food Director, *Good Housekeeping*

7

Introduction

Consider the casserole a cook's jackpot. Once you've assembled the ingredients in a baking dish and popped it in the oven, the heat's off the cook, leaving you free to enjoy the enticing aroma of a fabulous meal and/or dessert to come. Warm, comforting, and hearty, casseroles hit the sweet spot as the ultimate family-friendly meal: They're a cinch to pull off in a hurry—plus, many of our big-batch recipes guarantee you'll have leftovers for lunch or dinner the next day.

The word "casserole" literally refers to the cookware, which is most often glass, ceramic, or enameled cast-iron. As for which baking dish works best, Good Housekeeping casserole recipes specify the volume or dimensions of cookware. If you're not sure about the exact measurement of your baking dish, the capacity is sometimes printed or stamped under the dish. We also have a handy chart to use as a guide (see Sized to Fit, below). Many of our recipes also specify shallow casserole dishes. That means they should measure 2 inches (or less) in depth.

MEASURE FOR MEASURE

If you don't have the size of baking dish or Dutch oven called for in the recipe, don't panic—there's wiggle room!

DISH TOO SMALL?

Line the oven rack underneath with foil to catch any drips. Or cook the extras in a smaller baking dish. Both should be ready before the recommended cooking time is up.

DISH TOO BIG?

Relax, you can probably get away with it. But if you're making an egg-based recipe, like a strata or bread pudding, it's best to use the size called for, in order for the mixture to set properly.

Sized to Fit

DISH SIZE	APPROXIMATE VOLUME
8" by 8" glass or ceramic baking dish	1½ quarts
11" by 7" glass or ceramic baking dish	2 quarts
10" by 10" glass or ceramic baking dish	2½ quarts
13" by 9" glass or ceramic baking dish	3 quarts
15" by 10" glass or ceramic baking dish	4 quarts

NOTE: If you have an oval or round casserole dish, use a liquid measuring cup and fill the dish with water to the rim, not the lip below it. For example, if a casserole holds 10 cups of water, it's a 2½-quart size.

THE DISH

Unlike stovetop cookware, variations in casserole dishes won't make a significant difference in the speed or success of a recipe. So glass, ceramic, and enameled cast-iron cookware can be used interchangeably. However, when it comes to style, there are choices:

TEMPERED GLASS (CLEAR OR TINTED) Economical; simple, neutral design coordinates with any tableware; freezer to oven safe; microwave and dishwasher safe; retains heat well.

CERAMIC Moderately priced; available in many styles; most can go from freezer to oven to dishwasher; retains heat well.

HANDMADE CERAMIC Moderate to pricey; beautiful oven-to-table ware for entertaining; may not withstand oven temperatures as high as glass or commercial ceramic; hand washing preferable; most suitable for freezing and microwaving; may not retain heat as well as glass or commercial ceramic.

ENAMELED CAST-IRON Moderate to highly priced; available in bright primary colors; flameproof and ovenproof, so you can brown ingredients on the stovetop prior to baking; highly durable (although the enamel can chip); hand wash; fine for the freezer, but not the microwave; retains heat well.

THE GOODS

Ready to roll? Before you do, know your ingredients. Here's a run-down on some common goods and how best to use them.

BREADCRUMBS For casseroles with crunch, dried breadcrumbs are a must-have item. We like dried unseasoned (versus seasoned) crumbs; they're less salty and provide a blank canvas to get creative with flavorings. Panko (Japanese-style breadcrumbs) can be swapped in for extra crunch. If you choose to make your own toasted breadcrumbs, start with good-quality artisan or sourdough bread. Or try whole wheat, multigrain, or rye bread. For extra texture and flavor, substitute a portion of the crumbs with finely chopped almonds, walnuts, pecans, or flax or sesame seeds.

BROTH In an ideal world you would have a freezer full of homemade stock, but for casseroles, good quality canned or aseptically packaged broth is a perfectly acceptable convenience. We prefer the cleaner taste of reduced-sodium broth, and if you want to go organic, the flavor is definitely worth the extra coin.

CANNED TOMATOES Tomatoes are canned within hours of being picked to best preserve their color and flavor, so when it comes to casseroles, they don't play second fiddle to fresh. Those varieties grown specifically for canning, like Roma and San Marzano, have a high flesh-to-juice ratio, making them ideal for sauce. Many crushed and diced canned tomatoes are thickened with tomato puree (made from cooked and strained tomatoes), which changes the flavor of a dish. So check the label.

CHEESE It's hard to imagine an ooey, gooey casserole without it. For best flavor and texture, prepare cheese as you go in your baked dish—whether the recipe calls for grated, shredded, or crumbled. Also experiment with more flavorful cheeses, like adding chopped smoked mozzarella to our Ziti with Eggplant & Ricotta (page 72).

Instead of grating a wedge of Parmesan, try piquant Pecorino Romano; sharp, tangy dry Jack; or manchego, the popular sheep's milk cheese from Spain.

DRIED HERBS AND SPICES Casseroles often rely on dried seasonings, as their flavor can stand up to longer cooking times. However, just like fresh, dried seasonings need some TLC. Store them in airtight containers in a cool, dry space, and away from the stove, dishwasher, sink, or a window. Under the right conditions, whole spices can be kept up to 4 years, ground spices up to 3 years, and dried herbs 1 to 3 years. Not sure if your seasonings are fresh? Check the color, as fading is a good indicator of flavor loss. Also, taste and smell your spices and herbs; if a fresh odor or taste is missing, it's time for a replacement.

EGGS Our recipes call for large eggs, but if you only have medium or extra-large, the majority of our recipes are flexible enough to use them interchangeably. However, if a recipe calls for 4 or more eggs and you only have medium, add an extra egg. (Or, if a recipe calls for more than 5 eggs and you only have extra-large, decrease the amount of eggs by 1.)

FROZEN PEAS (AND OTHER VEGGIES) Frozen peas are a casserole staple, but, like all frozen veggies, they contain lots of moisture, which can make your casserole soggy. So if a dish calls for frozen veggies, double check the recipe to make sure the vegetable is thawed. If so, thaw as the package directs, but add an extra step of patting the vegetable dry with paper towels.

PASTA Getting the right texture in a baked pasta dish can be tricky. The potential deal breaker: Once you close the oven door, pasta will continue to cook. Add it uncooked to a casserole and bake, and you'll wind up with crunch (and we're not talking about the crumb topping). Cook it as the label directs and then bake, and you'll end up with mush. So unless a recipe specifies otherwise, cook pasta 2 minutes less than the suggested cooking time on the package. You want cooked pasta to be very "al dente" before adding it to the casserole dish—after that, the oven will take care of the rest.

SERVE NOW, OR LATER

One of the biggest selling points of casseroles is that you can enjoy a hot and bubbly dish tonight, or freeze the baked casserole up to 3 months and reheat when you need it. Follow our game plan (below) for a fabulous meal in your future. Delayed gratification never tasted so good!

- Cool the baked casserole at room temperature 30 minutes, and then refrigerate 30 minutes.
- Wrap the baking dish tightly in foil or plastic wrap and freeze. Or, before making the casserole, line the baking dish with heavy-duty greased foil. Cool and chill as directed (above), then freeze until frozen solid. Remove frozen food and transfer to a large zip-tight plastic bag.
- Thaw the frozen casserole in the refrigerator until slightly thawed, at least 24 hours but no longer than 2 days. (If the casserole was frozen in a foil-lined baking dish, unwrap and slip it back into the baking dish to thaw.)

NOTE
Baked pasta dishes, and those containing cooked potatoes and/or some dairy products such as yogurt, are not ideal for freezing.

- Unwrap the thawed casserole and cover it loosely with foil. Bake at a slightly lower temperature than specified in the recipe for about 1 hour, then remove the foil and bake until the center of the casserole reaches 160°F on an instant-read thermometer, 20 to 30 minutes.
- To microwave, unwrap the casserole and cover the top of the microwave-safe dish with waxed paper or plastic wrap so the wrap does not touch the food, turning back one corner of the wrap to vent. Microwave on Low (30%) until the ice crystals are gone and you can easily insert a knife into the center of the casserole, about 10 minutes. Cover again and microwave on High until the food is heated through and the internal temperature of the casserole reaches 160°F, 15 to 20 minutes longer.

A MOVABLE FEAST

When it comes to taking your casserole on the road and keeping it piping hot, you have choices:

GRAB A FLAT-BOTTOMED BOX (OR A ROASTING PAN) and line it with a bath or beach towel. Place the casserole in the box and pack rolled or folded towels around the dish. Top it with more towels. The towels will provide insulation, prevent the dish from sliding, and soak up any spills during transit.

USE A COOLER—it keeps food hot too. Line the cooler with towels or potholders, tuck the dish in, then top the dish with more towels and close the lid.

BUY AN INSULATED CASSEROLE CARRIER especially if you attend a lot of potlucks. Prices start around $12.

Hot Dish Tips

Before you grab the potholders and dish up something delish, keep these smart hints at your fingertips!

1 Always grease the baking dish with oil or nonstick cooking spray. Not only will it prevent the food from sticking, you can skip the heavy scrubbing during clean-up.

2 If a recipe calls to cover the baking dish with foil, use nonstick foil or spray the underside with nonstick cooking spray. (Your cheese and/or crumb topping will thank you.)

3 To test a casserole for doneness, insert a small knife in the center. If the knife is hot to the touch, then the whole casserole will be hot too.

4 Double the amount of crumb topping and freeze the extras for another casserole. It's also tasty sprinkled over roasted veggies before baking.

5 If you plan to freeze a casserole, hold off on the crunchy toppings until serving day.

Corned Beef Hash
(page 19)

1 | A.M. Wonders

Wanted: A warming morning meal that's easy enough for a family breakfast, dressy enough for a company brunch, and generous enough to feed a hungry crew. Must be prepared the night before, so you won't be groggy and rushed before serving. Done! This collection of heavenly bread puddings, scrumptious French toast, cheesy stratas, classic hash, and more, is ready to pop in the oven in the time it takes you to make a cup of morning Joe. By the time the table is set, friends and family assembled, and you're ready for a second cup, breakfast is ready to roll.

Many morning casseroles are bread-based, so for an impromptu A.M. bake, stash an extra loaf in the freezer next time you shop. Crisp French bread is a casserole favorite—its subtle flavor pairs well with sweet or savory ingredients. Italian bread may be substituted.

SYRUPY BANANA-NUT
Overnight French Toast

Yum! Layers of French bread and ripe bananas nestle in a warm, vanilla-cinnamon custard. If that doesn't sound heavenly enough, we sprinkled the bottom of the baking dish with brown sugar and melted butter to create a fabulous caramel syrup after the casserole bakes.

ACTIVE TIME: 20 MINUTES **TOTAL TIME:** 1 HOUR 5 MINUTES PLUS CHILLING

MAKES: 8 MAIN-DISH SERVINGS

6 tablespoons butter or margarine

1½ cups packed light brown sugar

5 large ripe bananas, cut diagonally into ½-inch-thick slices

1 long loaf French or Italian bread (12 ounces), cut crosswise into 1-inch-thick slices

6 large eggs

2 cups whole milk

2 teaspoons vanilla extract

1 teaspoon ground cinnamon

½ cup sliced almonds or coarsely chopped walnuts or pecans

1 In microwave-safe small bowl, microwave butter on High until melted, 1 minute. Stir sugar into butter until moistened. With fingertips, press sugar mixture onto bottom of 13" by 9" glass or ceramic baking dish. (It's okay if mixture does not cover bottom.) Spread bananas over sugar mixture; top with bread slices, cut sides down.

2 In medium bowl, with wire whisk, beat eggs; whisk in milk, vanilla, and cinnamon. Slowly pour milk mixture over bread; press bread down to absorb egg mixture. Sprinkle with almonds. Cover with plastic wrap and refrigerate at least 2 hours or overnight.

3 Preheat oven to 350°F. Remove plastic wrap and bake until bread is golden brown and knife inserted in center comes out clean, 45 to 50 minutes. Let stand 10 minutes for easier serving.

EACH SERVING: ABOUT 570 CALORIES, 13G PROTEIN, 89G CARBOHYDRATE, 20G TOTAL FAT (11G SATURATED), 5G FIBER, 191MG CHOLESTEROL, 465MG SODIUM.

TIP

Instead of the bananas, swap in 3 to 4 very ripe sliced pears or peaches, or 1 cup dried cherries, cranberries, or raisins.

HAM & CHEDDAR
Strata

Strata is a layered dish of eggs, bread, cheese,
and sometimes herbs and meat. Dijon mustard gives
this casserole a boost of zingy flavor. Plus, deli-sliced ham
means you won't need to cook the meat.

ACTIVE TIME: 25 MINUTES **TOTAL TIME:** 1 HOUR 25 MINUTES PLUS CHILLING
MAKES: 6 MAIN-DISH SERVINGS

8   ounces thinly sliced deli ham

3   cups reduced-fat (2%) milk

7   large eggs

2   tablespoons Dijon mustard

1   teaspoon fresh thyme leaves, chopped

¼   teaspoon salt

¼   teaspoon ground black pepper

1   loaf French bread (about 12 ounces), cut into
    ¼-inch slices

8   ounces cheddar cheese, shredded (2 cups)

1   tablespoon snipped fresh chives

1 Spray shallow 2-quart baking dish with
nonstick cooking spray. Line dish with ham.
2 In large bowl, with wire whisk, beat milk, eggs,
mustard, thyme, salt, and pepper until blended.
3 Arrange half of bread slices, overlapping
slightly, on bottom of prepared baking dish.
Pour half of milk mixture over bread. Sprinkle
with half of cheddar. Repeat layering. Cover
baking dish with plastic wrap and refrigerate
at least 1 hour or overnight.
4 Preheat oven to 350°F. Remove plastic wrap
and bake until golden and knife inserted in center
comes out clean, 50 to 55 minutes. Let stand
5 minutes for easier serving. Sprinkle with chives.

....

EACH SERVING: ABOUT 525 CALORIES, 36G PROTEIN,
48G CARBOHYDRATE, 22G TOTAL FAT (12G SATURATED),
2G FIBER, 283MG CHOLESTEROL, 1,420MG SODIUM.

SAUSAGE-FONTINA
Strata

Sweet Italian sausage and fontina cheese makes this
dish the perfect pick for a hearty morning meal.
Using Italian (versus milder-tasting Danish or Swedish)
fontina is definitely a plus, as it's much creamier
when melted and has a luxuriously nutty flavor.

ACTIVE TIME: 20 MINUTES   **TOTAL TIME:** 1 HOUR 25 MINUTES PLUS CHILLING
MAKES: 6 MAIN-DISH SERVINGS

- 12 ounces sweet Italian sausage links, casings removed
- 6 large eggs
- 2 cups reduced-fat (2%) milk
- ¼ teaspoon salt
- ¼ teaspoon coarsely ground black pepper
- 8 slices firm white sandwich bread, toasted
- 6 ounces fontina cheese, shredded (1½ cups)
- ¼ cup loosely packed fresh parsley leaves, chopped

1 Grease 8" by 8" glass or shallow 1½-quart ceramic baking dish. In 12-inch nonstick skillet, cook sausage over medium heat, stirring and breaking it up with side of spoon, until browned, 13 to 14 minutes. Transfer to paper towels to drain.

2 Meanwhile, in 4-cup liquid measuring cup or medium bowl, with wire whisk, beat eggs, milk, salt, and pepper until blended.

3 Arrange 4 slices of bread in bottom of prepared baking dish, cutting slices to fit if necessary. Sprinkle with half of fontina and all the sausage. Cover with remaining bread. Slowly pour egg mixture over bread; press bread down to absorb egg mixture. Top with remaining fontina. Let strata stand at room temperature 15 minutes, or cover with plastic wrap and refrigerate overnight.

4 Preheat oven to 350°F. Remove plastic wrap and bake until puffed and golden and knife inserted in center comes out clean, about 40 minutes (if refrigerated, bake about 10 minutes longer). Let stand 10 minutes for easier serving. Sprinkle with parsley.

EACH SERVING: ABOUT 480 CALORIES, 27G PROTEIN, 22G CARBOHYDRATE, 29G TOTAL FAT (13G SATURATED), 1G FIBER, 290MG CHOLESTEROL, 915MG SODIUM.

 TIP

If you want to sub in a country-style loaf of bread, use 6 or 7 slices and cut them to fit in the dish.

CORNED BEEF
Hash

Have leftover cooked potatoes and corned beef from last night's dinner? Put them to good use the next morning in these single-serve casseroles. This recipe is also terrific with pastrami. For photo, see page 12.

ACTIVE TIME: 15 MINUTES   **TOTAL TIME:** 45 MINUTES
MAKES: 4 MAIN-DISH SERVINGS

2   tablespoons vegetable oil

1   medium green pepper, chopped

1   medium red onion, finely chopped

1/8   teaspoon salt

2   cups chopped cooked potatoes

2   cups chopped cooked corned beef

1/4   cup fresh basil leaves, chopped

4   large eggs

ground black pepper

1 Preheat oven to 450°F. Spray four shallow 2-cup baking dishes with nonstick cooking spray.

2 In 12-inch nonstick skillet, heat oil over medium-high heat until hot. Add green pepper, onion, and salt. Cook, stirring occasionally, until vegetables are almost tender, about 10 minutes.

3 Add cooked potatoes and cooked corned beef. Cook, stirring often, 5 minutes. Stir in basil. Divide among prepared baking dishes. Top each with 1 egg and pinch of black pepper. Bake until desired doneness, 13 to 15 minutes.

EACH SERVING: ABOUT 410 CALORIES, 21G PROTEIN, 21G CARBOHYDRATE, 27G TOTAL FAT (7G SATURATED), 3G FIBER, 255MG CHOLESTEROL, 915MG SODIUM.

TIP
For extra-buttery flavor, use cooked Yukon Gold potatoes.

ALMOND-OAT
Berry Bake

Old-fashioned oats, quinoa, and chia seeds
partner up with strawberries and blueberries
in a healthy morning bake that will
remind you of a best-of-summer fruit crisp.

ACTIVE TIME: 15 MINUTES **TOTAL TIME:** 1 HOUR 5 MINUTES
MAKES: 6 MAIN-DISH SERVINGS

2¾ cups low-fat (1%) milk

¼ cup melted butter

1   tablespoon vanilla extract

1   cup old-fashioned oats, uncooked

1   cup quinoa

½ cup roasted salted almonds, chopped

½ cup packed light brown sugar

3   tablespoons chia seeds

1   teaspoon baking powder

¼ teaspoon salt

1   cup blueberries

2   cups strawberries, hulled and quartered

vanilla low-fat yogurt, optional

1 Preheat oven to 375°F. Spray shallow 2-quart baking dish with nonstick cooking spray. Place on foil-lined cookie sheet.

2 In medium bowl, whisk together milk, melted butter, and vanilla until blended. In prepared baking dish, combine oats, quinoa, almonds, brown sugar, chia seeds, baking powder, and salt.

3 Pour milk mixture over dry ingredients in baking dish. Top with blueberries and strawberries. Bake until almost all liquid has been absorbed, about 45 minutes. Let stand 5 minutes for easier serving. Serve with yogurt, if using.

EACH SERVING: ABOUT 476 CALORIES, 14G PROTEIN, 64G CARBOHYDRATE, 19G TOTAL FAT (6G SATURATED), 8G FIBER, 26MG CHOLESTEROL, 364MG SODIUM.

TIP
No chia seeds? Substitute flax seeds (or try a combination of both).

HAM & CHEESE
Grits Casserole

Quick-cooking grits make this casserole a cinch to prep.
Pickled jalapeños provide the kick, but if you prefer
not to open a jar just for this recipe, omit the chile and use
pepper Jack instead of Monterey Jack cheese.

ACTIVE TIME: 25 MINUTES   **TOTAL TIME:** 1 HOUR 25 MINUTES
MAKES: 6 MAIN-DISH SERVINGS

3½ cups fat-free (skim) milk

1   teaspoon salt

1¼ cups quick-cooking grits

4   ounces cooked ham, diced (¾ cup)

3   ounces low-fat Monterey Jack cheese,
    shredded (¾ cup)

2   tablespoons freshly grated Parmesan cheese

1   pickled jalapeño chile, minced

2   large eggs

3   large egg whites

1 Preheat oven to 325°F. Grease shallow 2-quart baking dish. In heavy 3-quart saucepan, heat 1½ cups milk, *2¼ cups water*, and salt to boiling over medium-high heat. Gradually stir in grits, beating constantly with whisk. Reduce heat to low; cover and simmer, stirring occasionally, 5 minutes. Remove saucepan from heat; stir in ham, Monterey Jack, Parmesan, and jalapeño.
2 In large bowl, with wire whisk, beat eggs, egg whites, and remaining 2 cups milk until blended. Gradually add grits to egg mixture (mixture will be lumpy).
3 Pour mixture into prepared baking dish. Bake until top is set and edges are lightly golden, 45 to 50 minutes. Let stand 10 minutes for easier serving.

EACH SERVING: ABOUT 300 CALORIES, 19G PROTEIN, 34G CARBOHYDRATE, 9G TOTAL FAT (5G SATURATED), 2G FIBER, 98MG CHOLESTEROL, 870MG SODIUM.

TIP
Up the heat index by having a bottle of hot pepper sauce handy to accompany the dish.

CINNAMON-RAISIN
Overnight French Toast

This scrumptious brunch special has
an irresistible layer of caramelized apple slices
nestled between layers of cinnamon-raisin bread.
Serve with mimosas and you're good to go.

ACTIVE TIME: 45 MINUTES   **TOTAL TIME:** 1 HOUR 35 MINUTES PLUS CHILLING
MAKES: 12 MAIN-DISH SERVINGS

APPLE FILLING

2 tablespoons butter or margarine

4 Golden Delicious apples, cored, peeled, and
   sliced

¼ cup packed light brown sugar

3 tablespoons apple brandy (applejack) or
   apple juice

FRENCH TOAST

1 loaf (16 ounces) cinnamon-raisin bread

3 cups whole milk

½ teaspoon salt

½ teaspoon ground cinnamon

10 large eggs

1 tablespoon butter or margarine

2 tablespoons granulated sugar

1 Prepare Apple Filling: In 12-inch skillet, melt
butter over medium heat. Add apples and brown
sugar and cook, stirring occasionally, until apples
are deep golden, about 20 minutes. Stir in apple
brandy and cook 1 minute.

2 Prepare French Toast: Grease 13" by 9"
ceramic or glass baking dish. Arrange half of
bread slices, overlapping slightly, on bottom of
prepared baking dish.

3 In medium bowl, with wire whisk, beat milk,
salt, cinnamon, and eggs until blended. Pour half
of egg mixture over bread. Reserve one-fourth
of apple filling; cover and refrigerate to spoon
on casserole after baking. Spread remaining
apple filling over bread in even layer. Arrange
remaining bread slices over apple layer. Pour
remaining egg mixture over bread; press bread
down to absorb egg mixture. Dot bread with
butter; sprinkle with granulated sugar. Cover
baking dish with plastic wrap and refrigerate
overnight.

4 Preheat oven to 325°F. Remove plastic wrap
and bake until knife inserted in center comes out
clean, 50 to 55 minutes. Reheat reserved apple
filling in microwave oven until heated through.
Serve with French toast.

EACH SERVING: ABOUT 260 CALORIES, 10G PROTEIN,
36G CARBOHYDRATE, 10G TOTAL FAT (3G SATURATED),
3G FIBER, 185MG CHOLESTEROL, 225MG SODIUM.

CHILES RELLENOS
Casserole

Traditional chiles rellenos are made from green chiles that are stuffed, breaded and fried, which can be a hassle (and not too healthy). We simplified matters by layering canned green chiles, sliced red pepper, and extra-sharp cheddar with beaten eggs and milk for a casserole that's bake-and-make easy.

ACTIVE TIME: 15 MINUTES **TOTAL TIME:** 40 MINUTES
MAKES: 4 MAIN-DISH SERVINGS

- 6 large eggs
- 1 cup reduced-fat (2%) milk
- 2 tablespoons all-purpose flour
- ¼ teaspoon sweet paprika
- ¼ teaspoon salt
- ½ teaspoon ground black pepper
- 2 cans (5¾ ounces each) whole green chiles, drained and thinly sliced
- 1 medium red pepper (8 to 10 ounces), cut into ¼-inch pieces
- 4 ounces extra-sharp cheddar cheese, shredded (1 cup)
- ½ cup packed fresh cilantro leaves, finely chopped

1 Preheat oven to 350°F. Grease shallow 2-quart ceramic or glass baking dish.

2 In large bowl, with wire whisk, beat eggs, milk, flour, paprika, salt, and black pepper until blended. Add chiles, red pepper, cheddar, and ¼ cup cilantro; pour into prepared baking dish.

3 Bake until puffed and golden brown and center still jiggles slightly, 35 to 40 minutes. Let stand 10 minutes for easier serving. Sprinkle with remaining ¼ cup cilantro.

....

EACH SERVING: ABOUT 305 CALORIES, 20G PROTEIN, 14G CARBOHYDRATE, 18G TOTAL FAT (9G SATURATED), 3G FIBER, 353MG CHOLESTEROL, 825MG SODIUM.

TIP

Punch up the flavor by adding 4 ounces chopped chorizo sausage along with the chiles in step 2.

SPINACH & JACK CHEESE
Bread Pudding

Bread puddings aren't just sweet, and thanks
to sliced sandwich bread and frozen chopped spinach,
there's no heavy knife work in this savory dish.
Try this recipe with crumbled feta or goat cheese if you like.

ACTIVE TIME: 15 MINUTES **TOTAL TIME:** 45 MINUTES
MAKES: 6 MAIN-DISH SERVINGS

6   large eggs

2   cups low-fat (1%) milk

¼   teaspoon dried thyme

¼   teaspoon salt

¼   teaspoon coarsely ground pepper

pinch ground nutmeg

1   package (10 ounces) frozen chopped
    spinach, thawed and squeezed dry

4   ounces Monterey Jack cheese, shredded
    (1 cup)

8   slices firm white bread, cut into ¾-inch
    pieces

1 Preheat oven to 375°F. In large bowl, with wire whisk, beat eggs, milk, thyme, salt, pepper, and nutmeg until blended. With rubber spatula, stir in spinach, Monterey Jack, and bread.

2 Pour mixture into 13" by 9" ceramic or glass baking dish. Bake until browned and puffed and knife inserted in center comes out clean, 20 to 25 minutes. Let stand 5 minutes for easier serving.

EACH SERVING: ABOUT 280 CALORIES, 17G PROTEIN,
22G CARBOHYDRATE, 13G TOTAL FAT (6G SATURATED),
2G FIBER, 233MG CHOLESTEROL, 545MG SODIUM.

TIP

Sub in your favorite frozen greens for the
spinach, such as chopped kale, collards, or
mustard greens.

Family Lasagna
(page 35)

2 | Classic Bakes

Welcome to the world of casseroles that never go out of style—with an important caveat: better taste. The reason? Our dishes hit all the nostalgic sweet spots, but leave the ubiquitous "cream of" soups behind. For example, take our Creamy Chicken & Mushroom Pie (page 30); it has a delicate white wine-mushroom sauce with fresh tarragon topped off with a puff pastry crust. Or a fabulous lasagna, updated with no-boil noodles and 5 kinds of veggies. No worries about the workload, as each of these all-time faves, like Tuna-Melt Casserole (page 37) and Layered Three-Bean Casserole (page 45), are just as convenient to throw in the oven as mama's.

Best of all, each classic casserole is an all-in-one beauty, with protein, veggies, and starch built right in. No multiple components to get a meal on the table. What could be more family-friendly?

CREAMY CHICKEN &
Mushroom Pie

For this fabulous pot pie, we start with frozen puff pastry
and bake it separately from the filling. The result:
a super-flaky crust that never gets soggy.

ACTIVE TIME: 35 MINUTES **TOTAL TIME:** 50 MINUTES
MAKES: 6 MAIN-DISH SERVINGS

1 sheet frozen puff pastry, thawed

1 tablespoon butter or margarine

1½ pounds chicken tenders, cut into 1-inch chunks

¼ teaspoon salt

¼ teaspoon ground black pepper

2 shallots, chopped

1 pound assorted mushrooms, sliced

3 carrots, thinly sliced (8 ounces)

⅓ cup dry white wine

¼ cup all-purpose flour

2 cups reduced-sodium chicken broth

¾ cup half-and-half or light cream

1 cup frozen peas, thawed

2 teaspoons chopped fresh tarragon

1 Preheat oven to 400°F. Unfold pastry; roll to size of 2½-quart baking dish. Invert dish over pastry; with knife, trim pastry to fit. Place pastry on cookie sheet; refrigerate.

2 In 12-inch skillet, melt ½ tablespoon butter over medium-high heat. Sprinkle chicken with salt and pepper. Add chicken to skillet and cook, stirring until browned, about 5 minutes; transfer to plate.

3 With fork, prick pastry all over. Bake until browned, 10 to 15 minutes.

4 Meanwhile, in same skillet, melt remaining ½ tablespoon butter over medium-high heat. Add shallots and cook, stirring, about 2 minutes. (If pan is dry, add *2 tablespoons water.*) Add mushrooms and carrots and cook, stirring, about 6 minutes. Add wine and bring to boil; boil until dry, about 2 minutes. Stir in flour, then broth; heat to boiling over high heat. Stir in chicken and juices. Reduce heat to medium and simmer until chicken is cooked through (165°F), about 5 minutes. Stir in half-and-half, peas, and tarragon; simmer 1 minute. Pour filling into baking dish; top with pastry.

EACH SERVING: ABOUT 430 CALORIES, 32G PROTEIN, 33G CARBOHYDRATE, 19G TOTAL FAT (6G SATURATED), 4G FIBER, 84MG CHOLESTEROL, 720MG SODIUM.

TIP

Save time by using 2 packages (8 ounces each) of sliced 'shrooms, like white and cremini or shiitake mushrooms.

SHEPHERD'S **Pie**

For a healthier take on this classic Greek bake,
we swapped lean ground beef for the lamb and doubled
the veggies. A touch of reduced-fat cream cheese gives
the potato topping a delicate creamy texture.

ACTIVE TIME: 50 MINUTES   **TOTAL TIME:** 1 HOUR 15 MINUTES
MAKES: 6 MAIN-DISH SERVINGS

- 2 pounds all-purpose potatoes, peeled and cut into quarters
- ½ cup low-fat (1%) milk
- 2 tablespoons reduced-fat cream cheese (Neufchâtel)
- ¾ teaspoon salt
- ½ teaspoon ground black pepper
- 1 pound extra-lean (97%) ground beef
- 2 large onions (10 to 12 ounces each), finely chopped
- 2 large carrots, finely chopped
- 2 large celery stalks, finely chopped
- ½ cup dry white wine
- 1½ teaspoons fresh thyme leaves, chopped
- 1 package (10 ounces) frozen peas, thawed
- 1 package (10 ounces) frozen corn, thawed

1 In 4-quart saucepan, place potatoes and enough *water* to cover; heat to boiling over high heat. Reduce heat to medium and simmer until potatoes are tender, about 18 minutes. Drain well; return to saucepan. Add milk, cream cheese, ¼ teaspoon salt, and ¼ teaspoon pepper; mash until smooth.

2 Preheat oven to 425°F. Heat 12-inch skillet over medium-high heat until hot. Add beef, ¼ teaspoon salt, and remaining ¼ teaspoon pepper; cook, stirring, until browned and cooked through, 3 to 5 minutes. With slotted spoon, transfer beef to large bowl.

3 To same skillet over medium-high heat, add onions, carrots, celery, and remaining ¼ teaspoon salt. Cook, stirring, until vegetables are tender, about 8 minutes. Add wine and cook until reduced by half, about 2 minutes. Stir in thyme and reserved beef with any juices.

4 In shallow 3-quart baking dish, spread half of potatoes in an even layer. Top with beef mixture, peas, and corn. Spoon remaining potatoes evenly on top; spread evenly to cover filling. Bake until top is golden brown, about 25 minutes.

EACH SERVING: ABOUT 350 CALORIES, 25G PROTEIN, 55G CARBOHYDRATE, 5G TOTAL FAT (2G SATURATED), 8G FIBER, 44MG CHOLESTEROL, 360MG SODIUM.

FIESTA NACHO
Casserole

Talk about easy! This pantry-friendly classic tosses
rotisserie chicken with tomatoes, salsa verde, corn, carrots,
and chili powder, then layers the chicken with
crunchy baked tortilla chips and crumbled feta cheese.

ACTIVE TIME: 20 MINUTES   **TOTAL TIME:** 40 MINUTES
MAKES: 4 MAIN-DISH SERVINGS

3 cups shredded rotisserie chicken breast
  meat

2 large tomatoes, chopped

1 cup shredded carrots

1 cup corn kernels

½ cup salsa verde

2 cloves garlic, crushed with garlic press

1 teaspoon chili powder

3 ounces baked whole-grain tortilla chips
  (about 28)

2 ounces feta cheese, crumbled (½ cup)

fresh cilantro leaves

hot pepper sauce

1 Preheat oven to 400°F. Spray shallow 2-quart
baking dish with nonstick cooking spray.

2 In large bowl, combine chicken, tomatoes,
carrots, corn, salsa, garlic, and chili powder.

3 In prepared baking dish, arrange one-third of
chips; top with half of chicken mixture, then half
of feta; repeat layering. Arrange remaining chips
on top. Bake until hot, about 20 minutes. Top
with cilantro. Serve with hot pepper sauce.

....

EACH SERVING: ABOUT 345 CALORIES, 32G PROTEIN,
35G CARBOHYDRATE, 10G TOTAL FAT (4G SATURATED),
4G FIBER, 92MG CHOLESTEROL, 855MG SODIUM.

FAMILY
Lasagna

Packed with zucchini, Swiss chard, tomatoes, and more,
this rendition of lasagna is not only a feast for the eyes—
it's also the perfect way to get your family to eat their veggies.
For photo, see page 28.

ACTIVE TIME: 25 MINUTES   **TOTAL TIME:** 1 HOUR 15 MINUTES
MAKES: 4 MAIN-DISH SERVINGS

2   medium zucchini or yellow summer squash, thinly sliced

3   teaspoons olive oil

¼   teaspoon salt

1   bunch Swiss chard, tough stems discarded, thinly sliced

1   small onion (4 to 6 ounces), finely chopped

2   cloves garlic, crushed with garlic press

1   teaspoon fresh thyme leaves, chopped

1   pound plum tomatoes, thinly sliced

4   oven-ready (no-boil) lasagna noodles

2   carrots, shredded

1   cup part-skim ricotta cheese

2   ounces provolone cheese, finely shredded

1 Arrange one oven rack 4 inches from broiler heat source and second rack in center. Preheat broiler.

2 In large bowl, toss zucchini with 1 teaspoon oil and ⅛ teaspoon salt. Arrange on 18" by 12" jelly-roll pan in single layer. Broil 6 minutes or until golden brown, turning over once. Set aside. Reset oven control to 425°F.

3 Rinse Swiss chard in cold water; drain, leaving some water clinging to leaves.

4 In 12-inch skillet, heat remaining 2 teaspoons oil over medium heat until hot. Add onion and cook, stirring occasionally, until softened, about 3 minutes. Add chard, garlic, thyme, and remaining ⅛ teaspoon salt. Cook, stirring frequently, until chard is very soft, 6 to 7 minutes. Remove skillet from heat and set aside.

5 In 8" by 8" shallow ceramic or glass baking dish, layer half of tomatoes, lasagna noodles, Swiss chard, shredded carrots, zucchini slices, and ricotta, in that order. Repeat layering once. Top with provolone. Cover baking dish with foil. (If making a day ahead, refrigerate.) Bake about 30 minutes (if refrigerated, bake about 10 minutes longer). Remove foil and bake until golden brown and bubbling, about 20 minutes longer.

EACH SERVING: ABOUT 310 CALORIES, 17G PROTEIN, 33G CARBOHYDRATE, 13G TOTAL FAT (6G SATURATED), 6G FIBER, 29MG CHOLESTEROL, 520MG SODIUM.

TUNA-MELT **Casserole**

This update on the sixties' elbow macaroni affair
stars corkscrew pasta, broccoli, and
a silky Swiss cheese sauce
topped off with juicy sliced tomatoes.

ACTIVE TIME: 40 MINUTES   **TOTAL TIME:** 1 HOUR
MAKES: 6 MAIN-DISH SERVINGS

1   package (16 ounces) corkscrew pasta

3   cups broccoli florets

2   tablespoons butter or margarine

2   tablespoons all-purpose flour

3/4 teaspoon salt

1/4 teaspoon ground black pepper

4   cups reduced-fat (2%) milk

4   ounces Swiss cheese, shredded (1 cup)

1   can (12 ounces) chunk light tuna in water,
    drained and flaked

2   medium tomatoes, cut into ½-inch-thick
    slices

1 Preheat oven to 400°F. Heat large covered
saucepot of *salted water* to boiling over high heat.
Add pasta and cook 5 minutes. Add broccoli to
pasta and cook until broccoli is tender and pasta
is al dente, 5 minutes. Drain well and return to
saucepot; set aside.

2 Meanwhile, in 3-quart saucepan, melt butter
over low heat. Stir in flour, salt, and pepper until
blended and cook, stirring, 1 minute. Gradually
stir in milk; increase heat to medium-high and
cook, stirring occasionally, until mixture thickens
and boils. Boil 1 minute, stirring frequently.
Remove saucepan from heat and stir in ½ cup
cheese until blended.

3 Add cheese sauce and tuna to pasta and
broccoli in saucepot; toss until evenly mixed.
Transfer mixture to shallow 3½-quart casserole
or 13" by 9" glass baking dish. Arrange tomato
slices on top, overlapping if necessary. Sprinkle
with remaining ½ cup cheese. Cover baking dish
with foil and bake until hot and bubbly, about
20 minutes.

EACH SERVING: ABOUT 570 CALORIES, 39G PROTEIN,
71G CARBOHYDRATE, 14G TOTAL FAT (6G SATURATED),
5G FIBER, 29MG CHOLESTEROL, 755MG SODIUM.

TIP

You can also use medium shell pasta instead
of the corkscrews.

SALMON **Noodle Bake**

Tender egg noodles, studded with chunks
of fresh salmon and peas, bake in an elegant
leek and mushroom cream sauce.

ACTIVE TIME: 25 MINUTES   **TOTAL TIME:** 45 MINUTES
MAKES: 6 MAIN-DISH SERVINGS

1½ cups low-fat (1%) milk

1 large leek (1 pound)

1 package (10 ounces) sliced mushrooms

1 tablespoon reduced-sodium soy sauce

2 tablespoons plus 1 teaspoon olive oil

2 large stalks celery, finely chopped

1 teaspoon fresh thyme leaves, chopped

3 tablespoons all-purpose flour

1 can (14 to 14½ ounces) reduced-sodium chicken broth (1¾ cups)

8 ounces curly egg noodles

12 ounces skinless salmon fillet, cut into 1-inch chunks

1 cup frozen peas

½ teaspoon salt

¼ teaspoon ground black pepper

⅓ cup panko (Japanese-style breadcrumbs)

1 Preheat oven to 350°F. Grease shallow 3-quart baking dish. Heat large covered saucepot of *salted water* to boiling over high heat. In glass measuring cup, microwave milk on High until warm, 2 minutes.

2 Meanwhile, trim and discard root and dark green top from leek. Discard any tough outer leaves. Cut leek lengthwise in half, then crosswise into ¼-inch-wide slices. Place leek in large bowl of *cold water*; with hand, swish to remove any sand.

Remove leek to colander. Repeat process with fresh water, changing water several times until sand is removed. Drain leek well and set aside.

3 In 12-inch skillet, combine mushrooms and soy sauce. Cook, stirring occasionally, over medium-high heat until mushrooms are tender and sauce evaporates, 5 to 6 minutes. Transfer to large bowl.

4 In same skillet, heat 2 tablespoons oil over medium-high heat until hot. Add leek, celery, and half of thyme. Cook, stirring occasionally, until golden and just tender, about 2 minutes. Add flour and cook, stirring, 1 minute. Continue stirring and add broth, then milk, in steady stream. Heat to boiling while stirring, then cook, stirring constantly, until thickened, about 2 minutes. Transfer to bowl with mushrooms.

5 While sauce cooks, add noodles to *boiling water*; cook 1 minute. Drain well.

6 To bowl with mushroom mixture, add noodles, salmon, peas, salt, and pepper. Gently stir to combine. Spread mixture evenly in prepared baking dish.

7 In small bowl, combine panko, remaining thyme, and remaining 1 teaspoon oil. Sprinkle evenly over top of noodle mixture. Bake until topping turns golden brown, 17 to 18 minutes.

EACH SERVING: ABOUT 370 CALORIES, 22G PROTEIN, 43G CARBOHYDRATE, 12G TOTAL FAT (2G SATURATED), 4G FIBER, 61MG CHOLESTEROL, 570MG SODIUM.

SPAGHETTI Pie

Call this carbonara-in-a-casserole
because it's got all the fixings: pasta, bacon, eggs,
and freshly grated Parmesan cheese.
Our addition of ricotta and milk makes it extra creamy.

ACTIVE TIME: 20 MINUTES **TOTAL TIME:** 1 HOUR
MAKES: 6 MAIN-DISH SERVINGS

1 package (16 ounces) spaghetti

4 slices bacon, chopped

1 large red onion (10 to 12 ounces), finely chopped

1 container (15 ounces) part-skim ricotta cheese

4 large eggs

2 cups reduced-fat (2%) milk

¼ teaspoon cayenne (ground red) pepper

1 cup freshly grated Parmesan cheese

¼ teaspoon salt

2 cups frozen peas

1 Preheat oven to 350°F.

2 Heat large covered saucepot of *salted water* to boiling over high heat. Cook spaghetti as label directs.

3 Meanwhile, in 12-inch skillet, cook bacon, stirring occasionally, over medium heat until crisp, 6 to 8 minutes. With slotted spoon, transfer bacon to paper towels to drain. To fat in pan, add onion. Cook, stirring occasionally, until tender, about 4 minutes.

4 While onion cooks, in very large bowl, whisk together ricotta, eggs, milk, cayenne pepper, ½ cup Parmesan, and salt.

5 Drain spaghetti well. Stir into ricotta mixture along with peas, bacon, and onion. Spread in even layer in shallow 3-quart baking dish. Sprinkle remaining ½ cup Parmesan on top. Bake until set, 30 to 35 minutes.

EACH SERVING: ABOUT 660 CALORIES, 36G PROTEIN, 76G CARBOHYDRATE, 23G TOTAL FAT (11G SATURATED), 6G FIBER, 175MG CHOLESTEROL, 700MG SODIUM.

COUNTRY **Captain**

The name of this curried chicken classic harks back
to the days when ships' captains in port cities
like Charleston, South Carolina, and Savannah, Georgia,
traded in spices from their travels abroad.

ACTIVE TIME: 20 MINUTES   **TOTAL TIME:** 45 MINUTES
MAKES: 6 MAIN-DISH SERVINGS

2   tablespoons vegetable oil

2   green onions, thinly sliced, plus additional
    for garnish

2   cups long-grain white rice

4   carrots, cut into ¼-inch half-moons

1   large sweet onion (12 to 14 ounces), finely
    chopped

1   large yellow pepper (8 to 10 ounces), finely
    chopped

2   cloves garlic, finely chopped

1   tablespoon grated peeled fresh ginger

1   tablespoon curry powder

1   teaspoon garam masala or ground cumin

2   cans (14½ ounces each) no-salt-added diced
    tomatoes, undrained

½   cup golden raisins

¼   teaspoon salt

¼   teaspoon ground black pepper

1½ pounds skinless, boneless chicken thighs

¼   cup sliced almonds, lightly toasted, for
    garnish

1 Preheat oven to 350°F.

2 In 7-quart Dutch oven or other heavy,
ovenproof pot with lid, heat 1 tablespoon oil over
medium-high heat until hot. Add green onions
and rice; cook, stirring, until onions soften, about
2 minutes. Add *3 cups water* and heat to boiling.
Cover and bake 15 minutes.

3 Meanwhile, in 12-inch skillet, heat remaining
1 tablespoon oil over medium-high heat until
hot. Add carrots, onion, yellow pepper, and
garlic. Cook, stirring occasionally, until golden
and tender, about 6 minutes. Add ginger, curry,
and garam masala; cook, stirring, 1 minute. Add
tomatoes and raisins. Heat to boiling.

4 Sprinkle chicken with salt and black pepper.
Add chicken to pot, submerging in vegetable
mixture. Heat mixture to boiling and cook
until chicken is cooked through (165°F), 2 to 4
minutes.

5 Uncover rice and pour chicken mixture over
top, spreading in even layer. Cover and bake until
bubbly, about 25 minutes. Garnish with almonds
and green onions.

EACH SERVING: ABOUT 575 CALORIES, 31G PROTEIN,
84G CARBOHYDRATE, 12G TOTAL FAT (2G SATURATED),
6G FIBER, 94MG CHOLESTEROL, 250MG SODIUM.

LAYERED THREE-BEAN
Casserole

Use your beans tonight! This scrumptious bake of black,
pink, and refried beans, layered with poblano peppers,
tortillas, salsa, Jack cheese, and sour cream, needs only
a simple green salad for the perfect casual meal.

ACTIVE TIME: 20 MINUTES   **TOTAL TIME:** 1 HOUR 30 MINUTES
MAKES: 6 MAIN-DISH SERVINGS

- 3 poblano peppers
- 1¼ cups reduced-fat sour cream
- ¼ cup low-fat (1%) milk
- 9 corn tortillas
- 2 cups salsa verde
- 1 can (15 ounces) low-sodium black beans, rinsed and drained
- 6 ounces Monterey Jack cheese, shredded (1½ cups)
- 1 can (16 ounces) refried beans
- 1 can (15 ounces) low-sodium pink beans, rinsed and drained
- ¼ small red onion, very thinly sliced
- ½ cup fresh cilantro sprigs

1 Arrange oven rack 5 inches from heat source.
Preheat broiler. In broiling pan lined with foil,
arrange poblano peppers in single layer. Broil
10 to 15 minutes or until blackened all over,
turning occasionally to evenly blacken. Wrap
peppers in foil; let cool.

2 Reset oven control to 350°F. Remove peppers
from foil; peel off skin and discard. Remove and
discard stems and seeds; thinly slice peppers.

3 In medium bowl, combine sour cream and
milk until blended. In 9" by 9" ceramic or glass
baking dish, arrange 3 tortillas in single layer,
tearing 1 tortilla in half to fit. Top with one-third
each of the salsa, the sour cream mixture, all of
the black beans, one-third of the cheese, and
one-third of the sliced poblano peppers, in that
order, spreading each in an even layer. Repeat
layering two more times, with refried beans in
center layer and pink beans on top. (If making
1 day ahead, cover and refrigerate.) Place baking
dish on jelly-roll pan to catch any drips. Bake,
uncovered, until mixture is bubbly and top
browns, 40 to 55 minutes.

4 Let stand 10 minutes for easier serving.
Sprinkle with onion slices and cilantro sprigs.

EACH SERVING: ABOUT 490 CALORIES, 24G PROTEIN,
65G CARBOHYDRATE, 16G TOTAL FAT (9G SATURATED),
12G FIBER, 47MG CHOLESTEROL, 890MG SODIUM.

TIP

You'll need a 16-ounce jar of salsa verde
for this zesty dish.

Chicken Enchilada Casserole
(page 51)

3 | Go Global

Hold the tuna! For nights when you're hungry and hankering for something a bit more exotic, tuck into a casserole with some serious international flair. You wouldn't necessarily think of a chicken-and-sweet potato bake with Thai green curry paste as a casserole, but our coconut chicken bake sets a new standard. Plus, if you're looking for more chicken dinners, we take the bird on a tasty tour through Greece and India.

We've also reimagined Italian classics as casseroles, like ravioli (morphed into lasagna!), Italian Wedding soup, and pasta e fagiole. Even beef stroganoff gets a casserole makeover. So grab your exotic seasonings and a baking dish—that's all you'll need for this culinary journey to a delicious destination.

COCONUT CHICKEN
Casserole

This Thai-inspired dish gets its kick from green curry paste,
a zesty mixture of lemongrass, galangal (Thai ginger),
green chiles, kaffir lime, coriander, cumin, and turmeric.
The addition of sweet potatoes helps tame the heat.

ACTIVE TIME: 25 MINUTES   **TOTAL TIME:** 45 MINUTES
MAKES: 6 MAIN-DISH SERVINGS

- 1 tablespoon vegetable oil
- 1½ pounds skinless, boneless chicken thighs, cut into 1½-inch chunks
- ½ teaspoon salt
- 1 medium onion, sliced
- 1 medium red pepper, cut into ¾-inch chunks
- 2 tablespoons green curry paste
- 2 teaspoons grated peeled fresh ginger
- 1 cup reduced-sodium chicken broth
- 1 large sweet potato, peeled and cut into ¾-inch chunks
- ¾ cup light coconut milk
- 1 teaspoon cornstarch
- 2 cups sugar snap peas, trimmed
- ½ cup fresh cilantro leaves

1 In 6-quart Dutch oven, heat oil over medium-high heat until hot. Sprinkle chicken with ¼ teaspoon salt. Add chicken to pot and cook, stirring, until browned, about 5 minutes. Transfer to medium bowl.

2 Add onion and red pepper to same pot. Cook, stirring, 3 minutes; stir in curry paste, ginger, and remaining ¼ teaspoon salt. Add broth and potato. Heat to boiling over high heat. Cover; cook 5 minutes. Stir in chicken. Reduce heat to medium; cover and simmer until chicken is cooked through (165°F) and vegetables are tender, about 10 minutes.

3 In another medium bowl, whisk together coconut milk and cornstarch until smooth; stir into pot along with peas. Heat to boiling over high heat. Reduce heat to medium; cover and simmer until peas are hot, about 3 minutes. Serve with cilantro over rice.

....

EACH SERVING (WITHOUT RICE): ABOUT 240 CALORIES, 24G PROTEIN, 14G CARBOHYDRATE, 9G TOTAL FAT (3G SATURATED), 3G FIBER, 94MG CHOLESTEROL, 475MG SODIUM.

TIP

Cook 1 cup jasmine or basmati rice as the label directs, then toss with chopped parsley to accompany this meal.

RAVIOLI & ZUCCHINI
Lasagna

This casserole looks and tastes like lasagna,
but thanks to cheese-filled ravioli, it takes
just minutes to assemble. Meat lovers will enjoy
the addition of ground beef in the sauce.

ACTIVE TIME: 20 MINUTES   **TOTAL TIME:** 55 MINUTES
MAKES: 6 MAIN-DISH SERVINGS

2   medium zucchini (about 1 pound total), cut lengthwise into ¼-inch-thick slices

1   package (26 ounces) frozen large cheese ravioli

3   teaspoons olive oil

1   small onion, chopped

8   ounces lean (90%) ground beef

1   jar (26 ounces) tomato-basil sauce

4   ounces part-skim mozzarella cheese, shredded (1 cup)

¼   cup freshly grated Parmesan cheese

1 Preheat oven to 375°F. Line cookie sheet with paper towels. Grease shallow 2-quart glass or ceramic baking dish.

2 Heat large covered saucepot of *water* to boiling over high heat. Add zucchini and cook 5 minutes. With tongs or slotted spoon, remove zucchini to prepared cookie sheet to drain. Return water to boiling. Add ravioli and cook until ravioli rise to top.

3 Meanwhile, in 3-quart saucepan, heat 2 teaspoons oil over medium heat until hot. Add onion and cook until tender and lightly browned, 8 to 10 minutes; transfer to small bowl. In same saucepan, heat remaining 1 teaspoon oil over medium-high heat until hot. Add beef and cook, breaking it up with side of spoon, until browned, 3 to 4 minutes. Stir in tomato sauce and onion; heat to boiling.

4 Drain ravioli; return to saucepot. Add meat sauce to ravioli in saucepot and stir until combined.

5 In prepared baking dish, arrange half of zucchini; top with half of ravioli, then half of mozzarella and half of Parmesan. Repeat layering of all ingredients. Bake until hot in the center and golden and bubbly on top, about 20 minutes.

EACH SERVING: ABOUT 455 CALORIES, 29G PROTEIN, 41G CARBOHYDRATE, 20G TOTAL FAT (10G SATURATED), 4G FIBER, 64MG CHOLESTEROL, 925MG SODIUM.

 TIP

Replace the beef with sweet or hot Italian sausage.

CHICKEN ENCHILADA
Casserole

This one-dish wonder calls for queso añejo or cotija. These aged Mexican cheeses are prized for their sharp flavor and firm texture, and are readily available in Hispanic markets. For photo, see page 46.

ACTIVE TIME: 20 MINUTES   **TOTAL TIME:** 1 HOUR
MAKES: 6 MAIN-DISH SERVINGS

2   tablespoons vegetable oil

1   pound chicken breast tenders, cut into ½-inch chunks

¼   teaspoon salt

¼   teaspoon ground black pepper

1   small red onion (4 to 6 ounces), thinly sliced

2   large zucchini, cut into 1½" by ½" spears

2   cups frozen corn kernels, thawed

2   cups salsa verde

½   cup reduced-fat sour cream

½   cup packed fresh cilantro leaves, chopped

12 corn tortillas

5   ounces queso añejo or cotija (aged Mexican cheeses) or feta cheese, crumbled (1 cup)

1 Preheat oven to 350°F. Grease shallow 3-quart baking dish.

2 In 12-inch skillet, heat 1 tablespoon oil over medium-high heat until hot. Sprinkle chicken with ⅛ teaspoon salt and ⅛ teaspoon pepper. Add chicken to skillet in single layer and sear 2 minutes. Turn chicken over; cook until just browned, 1 to 2 minutes. Transfer to large bowl.

3 Add onion and ¼ *cup water* to same skillet; cook 5 minutes or until tender, stirring and scraping pan. Add to chicken in bowl.

4 In same skillet, heat remaining 1 tablespoon oil until hot. Add zucchini, remaining ⅛ teaspoon salt, and remaining ⅛ teaspoon pepper. Cook, stirring occasionally, until browned and just tender, about 4 minutes. Transfer to bowl with chicken. To skillet, add corn and cook until browned, about 3 minutes. Transfer to bowl with chicken. Stir in salsa, sour cream, and half of cilantro until well mixed.

5 In prepared baking dish, arrange 4 tortillas in single layer. Spread evenly with one-third of chicken mixture and then one-third of cheese. Repeat layering twice.

6 Bake until hot, 20 to 25 minutes. Garnish with remaining cilantro.

EACH SERVING: ABOUT 460 CALORIES, 27G PROTEIN, 45G CARBOHYDRATE, 20G TOTAL FAT (7G SATURATED), 6G FIBER, 81MG CHOLESTEROL, 1,240MG SODIUM.

GREEK **Ziti Bake**

This show-stopping casserole, known as pastitsio
in Greece, features beef seasoned with tomatoes
and warm spices layered with tubular pasta
and a creamy cheese sauce.

ACTIVE TIME: 30 MINUTES **TOTAL TIME:** 1 HOUR 35 MINUTES
MAKES: 10 MAIN-DISH SERVINGS

- 1   tablespoon olive oil
- 1   large onion, chopped
- 1½ pounds lean (90%) ground beef
- 1¼ teaspoons salt
- ½   teaspoon ground black pepper
- 1   can (28 ounces) crushed tomatoes
- 1   tablespoon red wine vinegar
- ½   teaspoon pumpkin pie spice
- 1   package (16 ounces) ziti
- ½   cup (1 stick) butter
- ⅔   cup all-purpose flour
- 5   cups low-fat (1%) milk
- ¼   teaspoon ground nutmeg
- 3   large eggs, lightly beaten
- 1   cup freshly grated Parmesan cheese

1 Preheat oven to 375°F. Heat large covered
saucepot of *salted water* to boiling over high heat.
Spray shallow 3-quart baking dish with nonstick
cooking spray.

2 Meanwhile, in 12-inch skillet, heat oil over
medium-high heat until hot. Add onion and cook,
stirring, 4 minutes. Add beef, ½ teaspoon salt,
and pepper. Cook, stirring to break beef up with
side of spoon, until browned, about 5 minutes.

Add tomatoes, vinegar, and pie spice. Reduce
heat and cook 15 minutes.

3 Meanwhile, in 4-quart saucepot, melt butter
over medium-high heat. Stir in flour until
smooth. Slowly whisk in milk, nutmeg, and
remaining ¾ teaspoon salt. Reduce heat and
simmer, whisking, until thickened, 8 to 10
minutes. Cool 5 minutes. Whisk in eggs and
Parmesan.

4 Add ziti to *boiling water* and cook 2 minutes
less than label directs. Drain. Into prepared
baking dish, press half of ziti. Spread beef
mixture evenly over ziti. Layer on remaining ziti.
Top with sauce. Bake until top is browned and
edges are bubbly, about 45 minutes.

EACH SERVING: ABOUT 550 CALORIES, 31G PROTEIN,
54G CARBOHYDRATE, 23G TOTAL FAT (12G SATURATED),
4G FIBER, 138MG CHOLESTEROL, 800MG SODIUM.

TIP

Use a combo of equal parts Parmesan
and crumbled feta cheeses in the sauce,
if you like.

BEEF & PORTOBELLO
Stroganoff

We've taken the classic ingredients of Russian stroganoff—
mushrooms, sour cream, beef, and noodles—jazzed them up
with marjoram and caraway, then sprinkled the dish
with crunchy rye breadcrumbs.

ACTIVE TIME: 25 MINUTES **TOTAL TIME:** 55 MINUTES
MAKES: 6 MAIN-DISH SERVINGS

2   slices rye bread

2   tablespoons olive oil

1   large onion (10 to 12 ounces), finely chopped

2   stalks celery, finely chopped

1   pound lean (90%) ground beef

3/4   teaspoon salt

3/4   teaspoon ground black pepper

2   cloves garlic, finely chopped

1/2   teaspoon dried marjoram

1/4   teaspoon caraway seeds

12   ounces Portobello mushroom caps, thinly sliced

1/4   cup dry white wine

1   tablespoon cornstarch

1   can (14 to 14½ ounces) no-salt-added beef broth (1¾ cups)

12   ounces farfalle pasta

1/2   cup reduced-fat sour cream

chopped fresh flat-leaf parsley leaves, for garnish

1 Preheat oven to 400°F. Grease shallow 3-quart glass or ceramic baking dish. Heat large covered saucepot of *salted water* to boiling over high heat.

2 Meanwhile, tear bread into large chunks. In food processor with knife blade attached, pulse bread until crumbs form.

3 In 12-inch skillet, heat 1 tablespoon oil over medium-high heat until hot. Add onion and celery and cook, stirring, until golden brown, 3 to 4 minutes. Add beef, ¼ teaspoon salt, and ¼ teaspoon pepper. Cook, stirring to break beef up with side of spoon, until browned, 3 to 4 minutes. With slotted spoon, transfer mixture to large bowl.

4 To same skillet, add garlic, marjoram, and caraway. Cook until fragrant, about 15 seconds, then add mushrooms and *2 tablespoons water*. Cook, stirring frequently, until tender, about 4 minutes. Add wine, heat to boiling, and cook 2 minutes.

5 In small bowl, whisk together cornstarch and 1 tablespoon broth until smooth. Add remaining broth to skillet; heat to boiling. Stir in cornstarch mixture; cook, stirring occasionally, until thickened, 5 to 6 minutes.

6 Meanwhile, add pasta to *boiling water* and cook for half the time the label directs. Drain pasta well; transfer to bowl with meat mixture.

7 Stir sour cream, remaining ½ teaspoon salt, and remaining ½ teaspoon pepper into mushroom mixture in skillet; cook, stirring, until creamy, about 1 minute. Add to bowl with meat mixture and gently stir until mixed. Transfer to prepared baking dish and spread evenly.

8 In small bowl, combine crumbs and remaining 1 tablespoon oil. Sprinkle evenly over pasta mixture. Bake until crumbs are golden, 18 to 20 minutes. Garnish with parsley.

EACH SERVING: ABOUT 465 CALORIES, 25G PROTEIN, 66G CARBOHYDRATE, 13G TOTAL FAT (4G SATURATED), 8G FIBER, 82MG CHOLESTEROL, 765MG SODIUM.

ITALIAN WEDDING **Pasta**

For this easy-bake rendition of Italian Wedding Soup,
we've kept the two tastiest ingredients:
tiny meatballs and plenty of greens.

ACTIVE TIME: 30 MINUTES   **TOTAL TIME:** 50 MINUTES
MAKES: 8 MAIN-DISH SERVINGS

1   pound ground turkey

¼   cup plain dried breadcrumbs

¼   cup loosely packed fresh parsley leaves,
    chopped

1   clove garlic, crushed with garlic press

1   large egg

1   cup freshly grated Romano cheese

1   package (16 ounces) farfalle or bow tie pasta

1   tablespoon cornstarch

1½ cups reduced-fat (2%) milk

1   can (14 to 14½ ounces) reduced-sodium
    chicken broth (1¾ cups)

1   bag (9 ounces) baby spinach

¼   teaspoon ground black pepper

1 Preheat oven to 400°F. Line 15½" by 10½" jelly-roll pan with parchment paper or foil.

2 In medium bowl, with fingertips, mix turkey, breadcrumbs, parsley, garlic, egg, and ¼ cup Romano just until blended; do not overmix. Shape turkey mixture into thirty-six 1-inch meatballs; place in prepared pan. Bake meatballs 20 minutes.

3 Meanwhile, heat large covered saucepot of *salted water* to boiling over high heat. Add pasta and cook 2 minutes less than label directs. Drain pasta; return to saucepot.

4 In 2-cup liquid measuring cup, whisk cornstarch into milk. Add milk mixture and broth to pasta in saucepot; heat to boiling over medium-high heat, stirring frequently. Boil until sauce thickens slightly, about 1 minute. Remove saucepot from heat; stir in spinach, ½ cup Romano, and pepper. Add meatballs and gently toss to combine. Transfer pasta mixture to shallow 3-quart glass or ceramic baking dish; sprinkle with remaining ¼ cup Romano. Bake until hot in the center and golden brown on top, about 20 minutes.

EACH SERVING: ABOUT 390 CALORIES, 25G PROTEIN, 49G CARBOHYDRATE, 10G TOTAL FAT (4G SATURATED), 4G FIBER, 85MG CHOLESTEROL, 380MG SODIUM.

INDIAN CHICKEN &
Rice Casserole

Classically known as biryani, this gently spiced rice casserole, layered with meat and vegetables, is often served at family dinners. Up the wow factor by serving this dish with all the traditional garnishes.

ACTIVE TIME: 30 MINUTES   **TOTAL TIME:** 1 HOUR 10 MINUTES
MAKES: 6 MAIN-DISH SERVINGS

1   can (14 to 14½ ounces) chicken broth (1¾ cups)

1   cup basmati rice

3   cloves garlic, peeled

1   piece (½-inch) peeled fresh ginger, coarsely chopped

¼   cup sweetened flaked coconut

1   large onion, cut lengthwise in half and thinly sliced

3   teaspoons vegetable oil

1   small red pepper, cut into ½-inch pieces

1   pound skinless, boneless chicken breast halves, cut into ½-inch pieces

¾   teaspoon ground cumin

¾   teaspoon ground coriander

½   teaspoon salt

⅛   teaspoon cayenne (ground red) pepper

2   cups cauliflower florets, cut into ½-inch pieces

1   package (10 ounces) frozen peas and carrots

1   can (14½ ounces) diced tomatoes

1   cup plain fat-free yogurt

raisins, toasted sliced almonds, and toasted sweetened coconut, for garnish, optional

1 Preheat oven to 350°F. In 2-cup measuring cup, add enough *water* to chicken broth to equal 2 cups liquid. In 2-quart saucepan, heat chicken broth mixture to boiling over high heat. Place rice in shallow 2½-quart baking dish; stir in boiling broth mixture. Cover baking dish tightly with foil and bake until rice is tender and all liquid is absorbed, about 20 minutes. Remove baking dish from oven; set aside.

2 Meanwhile, in food processor with knife blade attached or in blender at medium speed, blend garlic, ginger, coconut, and half of onion until a paste forms; set aside.

3 In 12-inch nonstick skillet, heat 2 teaspoons oil over medium heat until hot. Add red pepper and remaining onion and cook, stirring, until golden, about 10 minutes. With slotted spoon, transfer vegetables to large bowl.

4 Add garlic mixture to skillet and cook, stirring, until golden, 8 to 10 minutes. Add chicken and remaining 1 teaspoon oil and cook, stirring occasionally, until chicken is lightly browned and cooked through (165°F). Add cumin, coriander, salt, and cayenne pepper, and cook 2 minutes. Transfer chicken mixture to bowl with vegetables.

5 To same skillet, add cauliflower and ¾ *cup water*; heat to boiling over high heat. Reduce heat to low; cover and simmer 3 minutes. Add peas and carrots and tomatoes with their juice; heat to boiling over high heat. Reduce heat to low; uncover and cook until cauliflower is tender and peas and carrots are heated through, about 2 minutes. Transfer cauliflower mixture to bowl with chicken. Stir in yogurt until well mixed.

6 With fork, fluff rice. Top cooked rice with chicken mixture. Bake uncovered until heated through, about 15 minutes. Garnish with raisins, almonds, and toasted coconut, if you like.

EACH SERVING (WITHOUT GARNISHES): ABOUT 335 CALORIES, 28G PROTEIN, 45G CARBOHYDRATE, 6G TOTAL FAT (2G SATURATED), 5G FIBER, 45MG CHOLESTEROL, 760MG SODIUM.

BAKED PASTA E
Fagioli

We turned pasta e fagioli, the beloved Italian bean soup,
into a casserole by adding spinach, topping it with sharp grated
Romano cheese, and baking it until golden and bubbly.
Pssst! You can still eat it with a spoon.

ACTIVE TIME: 20 MINUTES **TOTAL TIME:** 35 MINUTES
MAKES: 6 MAIN-DISH SERVINGS

8   ounces mini penne or elbow pasta
    (about 2 cups)
1   can (28 ounces) whole tomatoes in puree
1   tablespoon olive oil
1   medium onion, chopped
1   stalk celery, chopped
2   cloves garlic, crushed with garlic press
2   cans (15 to 19 ounces each) navy or other
    small white beans, rinsed and drained
1   cup reduced-sodium chicken broth
¼   teaspoon ground black pepper
1   package (10 ounces) frozen chopped
    spinach, thawed and squeezed dry
½   cup freshly grated Romano cheese

1 Preheat oven to 400°F. Heat large covered
saucepot of *salted water* to boiling over high heat.
Add pasta and cook 2 minutes less than label
directs. Drain pasta, reserving ¼ *cup cooking
water.* Return pasta to saucepot.
2 Meanwhile, drain tomatoes, reserving puree.
Coarsely chop tomatoes.

3 In 4-quart saucepan, heat oil over medium heat
until hot. Add onion and celery and cook, stirring
occasionally, until tender, 9 to 10 minutes. Add
garlic and cook 1 minute.
4 Stir in tomatoes with their puree, beans,
broth, and pepper; heat to boiling over high heat.
Reduce heat to medium; stir in spinach.
5 Add bean mixture, reserved *pasta cooking
water*, and ¼ cup Romano to pasta in saucepot
and toss until well mixed. Transfer pasta mixture
to shallow 3-quart glass or ceramic baking
dish. Sprinkle with remaining ¼ cup Romano.
Bake until center is hot and top is golden, about
15 minutes.

EACH SERVING: ABOUT 350 CALORIES, 20G PROTEIN,
65G CARBOHYDRATE, 6G TOTAL FAT (2G SATURATED),
12G FIBER, 7MG CHOLESTEROL, 945MG SODIUM.

TIP
Wrap a clean kitchen towel around thawed
frozen spinach to squeeze out the extra
moisture.

Green Bean–Cheddar
Casserole (page 75)

4 Veggie Pleasers

Amp veggies with a few basic fixings, bake and . . . Voila! You've got a satisfying meatless meal. Plus, they make an ideal side dish for every occasion, from potlucks, to barbecues, to holiday feasts. More than any other kind of casserole, veggie bakes flow with the season, an ideal way to enjoy a bumper crop of summer corn and tomatoes, like our Two-Cheese Corn Gratin (page 69), or sweet winter squash, such as our Butternut Squash Gratin (page 81)—plus other tasty options, including green beans, potatoes, and much more.

Fresh vegetables are high in moisture, so if the recipe specifies to cook them before baking, don't skip this step; otherwise, your casserole will be soggy. Besides, you can easily precook veggies and refrigerate them in an airtight container a couple of days before assembling your casserole. So simple.

MEATLESS **Chili**

A trio of beans—red kidney, white kidney, and black—
along with 5 kinds of veggies, bake in a smoky
chipotle-tomato sauce for a robust chili so satisfying
you won't miss the meat.

ACTIVE TIME: 30 MINUTES   **TOTAL TIME:** 2 HOURS PLUS STANDING
MAKES: 6 MAIN-DISH SERVINGS

1½ pounds mixed dried beans such as red
kidney, white kidney (cannellini), and black
(3 cups total), picked over

1   tablespoon vegetable oil

3   medium carrots, cut into ¼-inch slices

2   medium onions, finely chopped

1   celery stalk, finely chopped

1   medium red pepper, finely chopped

3   cloves garlic, minced

1   jalapeño chile with seeds, minced

2   teaspoons ground cumin

½   teaspoon ground coriander

1   can (28 ounces) tomatoes in puree

1   chipotle chile, canned in adobo sauce,
minced

2   teaspoons salt

¼   teaspoon dried oregano

1   package (10 ounces) frozen corn

1¼ cups loosely packed fresh cilantro leaves
and stems, chopped

1 In large bowl, place beans and add *cold water*
to cover by 2 inches. Let stand for 8 hours.

2 Drain soaking liquid from beans. In 5-quart
Dutch oven, place beans and *8 cups cold water*;
heat to boiling over high heat. Cover pot and
cook 1 hour or until beans are tender, stirring
occasionally. Drain beans and return to pot.

3 Meanwhile, in 10-inch skillet, heat oil over
medium heat until hot. Add carrots, onions,
celery, and red pepper and cook, stirring
frequently, until vegetables are tender, about
10 minutes. Stir in garlic, jalapeño, cumin, and
coriander; cook, stirring, 30 seconds. Stir in
tomatoes with their puree, chipotle chile, salt,
and oregano, breaking up tomatoes with side of
spoon; heat to boiling over high heat. Reduce heat
to low; simmer 10 minutes.

4 Stir tomato mixture, corn, and *2 cups water*
into beans. Cover pot and cook 30 minutes.
Remove pot from heat; stir in cilantro.

EACH SERVING: ABOUT 360 CALORIES, 20G PROTEIN,
66G CARBOHYDRATE, 4G TOTAL FAT (0G SATURATED),
11G FIBER, 0MG CHOLESTEROL, 1,195MG SODIUM.

CAULIFLOWER
Mac 'n' Cheese

As colorful as it is cheesy, veggie fans are going to love
this scrumptious mac studded with cauliflower, carrots, broccoli,
and topped off with tomatoes—and more cheese!

ACTIVE TIME: 30 MINUTES   **TOTAL TIME:** 1 HOUR 30 MINUTES
MAKES: 6 MAIN-DISH SERVINGS

1   medium head cauliflower (1½ pounds), core discarded, florets cut into 2-inch pieces

4   medium carrots (10 ounces), thinly sliced

1   cup no-salt-added vegetable broth

¼   cup reduced-fat cream cheese (Neufchâtel)

1   teaspoon Dijon mustard

pinch cayenne (ground red) pepper

3   ounces Gruyère cheese, shredded (¾ cup)

½   teaspoon salt

¼   teaspoon ground black pepper

12   ounces elbow macaroni

8   ounces small broccoli florets (3 cups)

2   medium plum tomatoes, seeded and chopped

¼   cup freshly grated Parmesan cheese

1 Preheat oven to 400°F. Heat covered 8-quart saucepot of *salted water* to boiling over high heat.

2 Add cauliflower and carrots to boiling water. Cook until very tender, about 15 minutes.

3 Meanwhile, in blender, combine broth, cream cheese, mustard, cayenne pepper, ½ cup Gruyère, salt, and black pepper. With slotted spoon, transfer vegetables to blender. Puree until very smooth.

4 Add pasta to same saucepot of *boiling water*. Cook half the time that label directs, adding broccoli during last minute of cooking. Drain; return to pot. Stir in cauliflower sauce and half of tomatoes. Spread evenly in shallow 2½-quart baking dish. Top with remaining cheeses and tomatoes.

5 Bake until golden brown on top and heated through, about 35 minutes.

....

EACH SERVING: ABOUT 345 CALORIES, 16G PROTEIN, 53G CARBOHYDRATE, 9G TOTAL FAT (5G SATURATED), 5G FIBER, 25MG CHOLESTEROL, 480MG SODIUM.

TWO-CHEESE
Corn Gratin

If you're looking to put a bumper crop of summer veggies to good use, this delicious bake of roasted yellow squash, tomatoes, fresh corn, and cheesy custard with basil is the meal ticket.

ACTIVE TIME: 35 MINUTES   **TOTAL TIME:** 1 HOUR 15 MINUTES
MAKES: 6 MAIN-DISH SERVINGS

1   pound yellow squash, cut into ¼-inch-thick slices

1   pound ripe tomatoes, halved, seeded, and cut into ⅓-inch-thick slices

2   tablespoons olive oil

½   teaspoon salt

ground black pepper

2   tablespoons chopped fresh basil

1½   cups whole milk

2   tablespoons cornstarch

3   large eggs

¼   cup snipped fresh chives

5   ears corn

¾   cup panko (Japanese-style breadcrumbs)

3   ounces extra-sharp cheddar cheese, shredded (¾ cup)

2   ounces mozzarella cheese, shredded (½ cup)

1 Preheat oven to 400°F. Grease shallow 3-quart baking dish.

2 Arrange squash and half of tomatoes in single layer, overlapping, in prepared baking dish. Drizzle with half of oil; sprinkle with ¼ teaspoon salt, ⅛ teaspoon pepper, and half of basil. Roast until vegetables are slightly dry, about 25 minutes.

3 Meanwhile, in large bowl, whisk together milk, cornstarch, ⅛ teaspoon salt, and ⅛ teaspoon pepper until cornstarch dissolves. Whisk in eggs and half of chives until blended.

4 Cut corn kernels from cobs. In medium bowl, combine panko, ¼ cup cheddar, remaining ⅛ teaspoon salt, remaining ⅛ teaspoon pepper, and remaining basil, chives, and oil.

5 Sprinkle remaining cheeses evenly over roasted vegetables. Top with corn; pour milk mixture over all. Place raw tomatoes around edge, slightly overlapping. Sprinkle panko mixture evenly over top.

6 Bake until browned and knife inserted in center comes out clean, 25 to 30 minutes. Let stand 10 minutes for easier serving.

....

EACH SERVING: ABOUT 365 CALORIES, 16G PROTEIN, 37G CARBOHYDRATE, 19G TOTAL FAT (7G SATURATED), 4G FIBER, 122MG CHOLESTEROL, 450MG SODIUM.

TIP

Fresh plum tomatoes, with their meaty flesh and low moisture content, are ideal for this recipe.

CABBAGE & BULGUR
Casserole

Napa cabbage is layered with a savory mixture of bulgur and diced veggies, then topped off with an Asian-inspired tomato sauce.

ACTIVE TIME: 45 MINUTES   **TOTAL TIME:** 1 HOUR 25 MINUTES
MAKES: 6 MAIN-DISH SERVINGS

1½ cups bulgur

1   tablespoon vegetable oil

2   medium carrots, diced

2   medium celery stalks, diced

1   medium red pepper, diced

½   small head Napa (Chinese) cabbage, about 1¾ pounds, cut crosswise into 2-inch pieces (about 12 cups leafy tops and 2 cups crunchy stems)

2   cloves garlic, crushed with garlic press

3   green onions, sliced

2   tablespoons minced, peeled fresh ginger

2   tablespoons plus 1 teaspoon soy sauce

2   tablespoons seasoned rice vinegar

1   can (14½ ounces) diced tomatoes

2   tablespoons light brown sugar

2   tablespoons chopped fresh parsley, for garnish

1 Preheat oven to 375°F. In 2-quart saucepan, heat *1½ cups water* to boiling over high heat; stir in bulgur. Remove pan from heat; cover and set aside.

2 In 5-quart Dutch oven, heat oil over medium-high heat until hot. Add carrots, celery, and red pepper; cook 5 minutes. Add cabbage stems and cook until vegetables are tender, about 7 minutes.

3 Reduce heat to low; add garlic, green onions, and ginger; cook, stirring, 1 minute. Add *½ cup water*; heat to boiling over high heat. Reduce the heat to low; simmer, stirring, 1 minute. Remove Dutch oven from heat; stir in 2 tablespoons soy sauce, 1 tablespoon vinegar, and cooked bulgur.

4 In small bowl, combine tomatoes with their juice, brown sugar, remaining 1 tablespoon vinegar, and remaining 1 teaspoon soy sauce.

5 In shallow 3-quart baking dish, place half of cabbage leaves; top with bulgur mixture, then remaining cabbage leaves. Spoon tomato mixture on top. Cover baking dish with foil and bake until hot in the center and top layer of cabbage leaves are wilted, about 40 minutes. Garnish with parsley.

EACH SERVING: ABOUT 220 CALORIES, 7G PROTEIN, 43G CARBOHYDRATE, 3G TOTAL FAT (0G SATURATED), 8G FIBER, 0MG CHOLESTEROL, 800MG SODIUM.

ZITI WITH
Eggplant & Ricotta

If you love eggplant parm, but not the idea of frying,
consider this pasta bake with roasted eggplant
for your next Meatless Monday.

ACTIVE TIME: 40 MINUTES   **TOTAL TIME:** 1 HOUR
MAKES: 6 MAIN-DISH SERVINGS

1   medium eggplant (about 1½ pounds),
    cut into 1-inch pieces

3   tablespoons olive oil

3/4 teaspoon salt

1   small onion, finely chopped

2   cloves garlic, minced

1   can (28 ounces) plum tomatoes in juice

2   tablespoons tomato paste

1/4 teaspoon ground black pepper

3   tablespoons chopped fresh basil leaves

1   package (16 ounces) ziti or penne

1/4 cup freshly grated Parmesan cheese

1   cup ricotta cheese

1 Preheat oven to 450°F. In large bowl, toss
eggplant, 2 tablespoons oil, and ¼ teaspoon salt
until evenly coated. Arrange eggplant in single
layer in two 15½" by 10½" jelly-roll pans or 2
large cookie sheets. Place pans with eggplant on
2 oven racks in oven. Roast eggplant until tender
and golden, about 30 minutes, rotating pans
between upper and lower racks halfway through
cooking, stirring twice. Remove eggplant from
oven; set aside. Turn oven control to 400°F.

2 Meanwhile, in 3-quart saucepan, heat
remaining 1 tablespoon oil over medium
heat until hot. Add onion and cook, stirring
occasionally, until tender, about 5 minutes. Add
garlic and cook, stirring frequently, 1 minute.
3 Stir in tomatoes with their juice, tomato paste,
pepper, and remaining ½ teaspoon salt, breaking
up tomatoes with side of spoon; heat to boiling
over high heat. Reduce heat to low and simmer
until sauce thickens slightly, about 10 minutes.
Stir in 2 tablespoons basil.
4 In large saucepot, prepare pasta in *boiling
salted water* as label directs. Drain; return pasta
to saucepot.
5 To pasta in saucepot, add roasted eggplant,
tomato sauce, and Parmesan; toss until evenly
mixed. Spoon mixture into six 2-cup gratin
dishes or shallow baking dishes; top with dollops
of ricotta.
6 Cover dishes with foil and bake 20 minutes
or until hot and bubbly. Sprinkle tops with
remaining 1 tablespoon basil.

....

EACH SERVING: ABOUT 500 CALORIES, 19G PROTEIN,
73G CARBOHYDRATE, 15G TOTAL FAT (5G SATURATED),
2G FIBER, 24MG CHOLESTEROL, 695MG SODIUM.

BAKED **Ratatouille**

Traditional ratatouille requires time-consuming stovetop cooking. Instead, we layer thinly sliced veggies in a casserole dish, drizzle them with a garlicky herb oil, and bake.

ACTIVE TIME: 25 MINUTES **TOTAL TIME:** 1 HOUR 15 MINUTES
MAKES: 8 SIDE-DISH SERVINGS

¼   cup olive oil

2   cloves garlic, crushed with garlic press

¾   teaspoon salt

½   teaspoon dried rosemary, crumbled

¼   teaspoon coarsely ground black pepper

1   small eggplant (about 1¼ pounds), cut crosswise into ¼-inch-thick slices

3   plum tomatoes (about 3 ounces each), cut crosswise into ¼-inch-thick slices

2   small zucchini (about 8 ounces each), cut diagonally into ¼-inch-thick slices

4   red potatoes (about 1 pound), cut into ⅛-inch-thick slices

1 Preheat oven to 425°F. In small bowl, stir together oil, garlic, salt, rosemary, and pepper until blended; set aside.

2 In 15" by 10" glass or ceramic baking dish or shallow 4-quart casserole dish, arrange half of eggplant slices crosswise in a row, overlapping slices slightly. Arrange rows of half of tomatoes, half of zucchini, and all of potatoes, overlapping slices and rows slightly. Repeat rows with remaining vegetables. (For vegetables to fit, they will almost be standing on their edges.) Drizzle olive-oil mixture over vegetables.

3 Cover baking dish with foil. Bake 15 minutes. Remove foil; bake until vegetables are tender and browned, about 35 minutes longer.

EACH SERVING: ABOUT 145 CALORIES, 3G PROTEIN, 20G CARBOHYDRATE, 7G TOTAL FAT (1G SATURATED), 4G FIBER, 0MG CHOLESTEROL, 230MG SODIUM.

TIP

Sub in 1 teaspoon chopped fresh rosemary for the dried.

GREEN BEAN–CHEDDAR
Casserole

Don't wait until the holidays to serve this easy spin
on a veggie classic—especially if you're looking to use up
leftover crusty bread. For photo, see page 62.

ACTIVE TIME: 30 MINUTES   **TOTAL TIME:** 1 HOUR 20 MINUTES
MAKES: 10 SIDE-DISH SERVINGS

3   pounds green beans, trimmed

2   cups stale bread, torn into small chunks

3   tablespoons olive oil

3   green onions, thinly sliced

3   tablespoons cornstarch

2½ cups whole milk

½   teaspoon salt

½   teaspoon ground black pepper

⅛   teaspoon ground nutmeg

8   ounces cheddar cheese, shredded (2 cups)

¼   cup finely grated Parmesan cheese

1 Preheat oven to 375°F.

2 Heat covered 7- to 8-quart saucepot of *salted water* to boiling over high heat. Add green beans and cook 2 minutes. Drain well; set aside.

3 In food processor with knife blade attached, pulse bread until coarse crumbs form. Transfer to medium bowl along with oil and green onions. Toss to combine; set aside.

4 In 4-quart saucepan, whisk together cornstarch and ½ cup milk until smooth. Add salt, pepper, and nutmeg. Slowly whisk in remaining 2 cups milk. Heat to boiling over medium-high heat, whisking frequently. Boil 2 minutes, whisking. Reduce heat to medium-low. Stir in cheeses one handful at a time, waiting until cheese melts before adding next handful.

5 Stir in green beans until well coated. Transfer mixture to shallow 3-quart baking dish. Top with reserved crumb mixture. Bake until crumbs are golden brown, 25 to 30 minutes.

EACH SERVING: ABOUT 245 CALORIES, 11G PROTEIN, 19G CARBOHYDRATE, 15G TOTAL FAT (7G SATURATED), 4G FIBER, 31MG CHOLESTEROL, 375MG SODIUM.

VEGGIE PLEASERS

SCALLOPED POTATOES
with Green Onions

We've updated this potato classic
by replacing the typical heavy cream with
a light white sauce studded with green onions.
(No worries—it tastes just as luscious!)

ACTIVE TIME: 30 MINUTES   **TOTAL TIME:** 1 HOUR 45 MINUTES

MAKES: 8 SIDE-DISH SERVINGS

3	tablespoons butter or margarine
1	bunch green onions
3	tablespoons all-purpose flour
2¾	cups whole milk
4	pounds all-purpose potatoes, peeled and thinly sliced
1	teaspoon salt
½	teaspoon ground black pepper
½	cup freshly grated Parmesan cheese

1 Preheat oven to 400°F. Lightly grease 13" by 9" glass or ceramic baking dish, or 2½-quart gratin dish.

2 Meanwhile, thinly slice green onions, reserving 2 tablespoons green tops.

3 In 5- to 6-quart saucepot, melt butter over medium heat. Add sliced green onions and cook, stirring occasionally, until tender, about 5 minutes. Add flour and cook, stirring constantly, 1 minute. Slowly whisk in milk. Cook, stirring constantly, until mixture boils and thickens, 6 to 7 minutes. Stir in potatoes, salt, and pepper. Cook, stirring gently, 5 minutes; remove saucepot from heat.

4 Transfer potato mixture to prepared baking dish, spreading evenly; sprinkle with Parmesan. Cover with foil sprayed with nonstick cooking spray, and bake 1 hour. Remove foil; reset oven control to broil. Broil, 6 inches from heat source, until Parmesan is golden, about 5 minutes. Sprinkle with reserved green onions.

EACH SERVING: ABOUT 295 CALORIES, 9G PROTEIN, 47G CARBOHYDRATE, 9G TOTAL FAT (4G SATURATED), 3G FIBER, 15MG CHOLESTEROL, 485MG SODIUM.

TIP

For an extra layer of flavor, add a bay leaf along with the potatoes in step 3. Just be sure to remove the leaf before serving.

SWEET POTATO &
Apple Gratin

Layers of sweet potato and sautéed apples with
a crunchy pecan-crumb topping make this elegant side
a perfect trimming to serve with Thanksgiving turkey.

ACTIVE TIME: 40 MINUTES   **TOTAL TIME:** 1 HOUR 40 MINUTES
MAKES: 8 SIDE-DISH SERVINGS

SWEET POTATO LAYERS

2   **tablespoons butter or margarine**

3   **large Golden Delicious apples
    (about 1¼ pounds), cored, peeled, and
    cut into ¼-inch-thick slices**

1   **jumbo onion (12 ounces), cut in half
    and thinly sliced**

2   **tablespoons apple brandy (applejack)**

6   **medium sweet potatoes (about 2½ pounds)**

¾   **teaspoon salt**

¼   **teaspoon coarsely ground black pepper**

¼   **teaspoon ground nutmeg**

1   **cup apple cider or apple juice**

PECAN CRUMB TOPPING

2   **tablespoons butter or margarine**

3   **slices firm white bread, cut into ¼-inch
    pieces (about 1¾ cups)**

½   **cup pecans, coarsely chopped**

1 **Prepare Sweet Potato Layers:** Grease shallow
2½-quart baking dish. In 12-inch skillet, melt
butter over medium heat. Add apples and onion
and cook, stirring frequently, until tender and
golden, about 25 minutes. Stir in applejack; cook
1 minute. Remove skillet from heat.

2 Meanwhile, peel and thinly slice sweet
potatoes. In cup, mix salt, pepper, and nutmeg.

3 Arrange one-third of sweet potato slices,
overlapping, in prepared baking dish. Spoon
one-third of apple mixture over potatoes.
Sprinkle with one-third salt mixture. Repeat
layering 2 more times. Pour apple cider over
potato and apple layers. Cover baking dish with
foil. (If making ahead, refrigerate up to 1 day.)

4 **Prepare Pecan-Crumb Topping:** In nonstick
10-inch skillet, melt butter over medium heat.
Add bread pieces and pecans and cook, stirring
occasionally, until bread and pecans are lightly
toasted, 5 to 6 minutes. Cool crumb topping
completely. (If making ahead, transfer crumb
topping to small container; cover and set aside.)

5 Preheat oven to 400°F. Bake casserole, covered,
1 hour. Sprinkle with crumb topping just before
serving.

EACH SERVING: ABOUT 300 CALORIES, 4G PROTEIN,
50G CARBOHYDRATE, 11G TOTAL FAT (2G SATURATED),
5G FIBER, 0MG CHOLESTEROL, 335MG SODIUM.

NEW GREEN BEAN
Casserole

What's "new" about this casserole?
We slashed the fat and calories of the traditional dish,
and added a cheesy crumb topping.

ACTIVE TIME: 45 MINUTES   **TOTAL TIME:** 1 HOUR 15 MINUTES
MAKES: 12 SIDE-DISH SERVINGS

- 3 pounds green beans, trimmed and cut in half
- 4 large shallots
- 1 tablespoon olive oil
- 1½ cups coarse fresh breadcrumbs
- 1 teaspoon fresh thyme leaves, chopped
- ½ teaspoon salt
- ½ teaspoon ground black pepper
- 3 cups low-fat (1%) milk
- 3 tablespoons butter or margarine
- ¼ cup all-purpose flour
- ⅛ teaspoon freshly grated nutmeg
- ½ cup freshly grated Parmesan cheese

1 Preheat oven to 350°F.

2 Heat covered 8-quart saucepot of *salted water* to boiling over high heat. Add beans and cook, uncovered, 6 minutes or until bright green and just tender. Drain well and transfer to shallow 3-quart glass or ceramic baking dish.

3 Meanwhile, finely chop 2 shallots. Thinly slice remaining shallots; set aside. In 12-inch skillet, heat oil over medium heat until hot. Add chopped shallots and cook, stirring occasionally, until browned and tender, 4 to 7 minutes. Add breadcrumbs and cook, stirring, until dry and golden, about 2 minutes. Transfer mixture to large bowl. Stir in thyme, ¼ teaspoon salt, and ¼ teaspoon pepper.

4 In microwave-safe measuring cup, microwave milk on High until warm, 4 minutes.

5 Meanwhile, in same 12-inch skillet, melt butter over medium heat. Add sliced shallots and cook, stirring occasionally, until golden brown and tender, about 5 minutes. Add flour and cook, stirring, 2 minutes. Gradually pour milk into flour mixture in slow, steady stream, stirring constantly; heat to boiling, stirring. Stir until thickened (mixture should have the consistency of heavy cream), about 2 minutes. Stir in nutmeg, remaining ¼ teaspoon salt, and remaining ¼ teaspoon pepper.

6 Pour sauce over green beans; gently stir until green beans are evenly coated. Stir Parmesan into bread crumb mixture; spread evenly over green bean mixture in baking dish. Bake until bread crumbs are golden brown and sauce is bubbly, about 30 minutes.

EACH SERVING: ABOUT 145 CALORIES, 7G PROTEIN, 17G CARBOHYDRATE, 6G TOTAL FAT (2G SATURATED), 4G FIBER, 6MG CHOLESTEROL, 305MG SODIUM.

VEGGIE PLEASERS

BUTTERNUT SQUASH
Gratin

Sweet winter squash is topped with a savory topping
of panko, olive oil, Parmesan cheese, thyme,
and crushed red pepper.

ACTIVE TIME: 15 MINUTES   **TOTAL TIME:** 1 HOUR
MAKES: 6 SIDE-DISH SERVINGS

½   teaspoon salt

1   butternut squash (2 to 2½ pounds),
    peeled, seeded, and cut crosswise into
    ½-inch half-moons

¼   cup reduced-sodium chicken or vegetable
    broth

1   tablespoon butter or margarine, cut up

½   cup panko (Japanese-style breadcrumbs)

½   cup freshly grated Parmesan cheese

1   tablespoon olive oil

1   teaspoon fresh thyme leaves, chopped, plus
    sprigs for garnish

¼   teaspoon crushed red pepper, or to taste

1 Preheat oven to 400°F. Grease shallow 2-quart baking dish.

2 Sprinkle ¼ teaspoon salt all over squash. In prepared baking dish, arrange squash in overlapping layers; pour broth into dish. Dot squash with butter. Cover tightly with foil and bake until knife pierces through squash with only slight resistance, about 35 minutes.

3 Meanwhile, in small bowl, combine panko, Parmesan, oil, thyme, crushed red pepper, and remaining ¼ teaspoon salt until mixed.

4 Remove foil and sprinkle squash evenly with panko mixture. Bake until crumbs are golden brown, 12 to 15 minutes longer. Garnish with thyme sprigs.

EACH SERVING: ABOUT 160 CALORIES, 5G PROTEIN, 21G CARBOHYDRATE, 7G TOTAL FAT (2G SATURATED), 4G FIBER, 6MG CHOLESTEROL, 365MG SODIUM.

POTATO **Kugel**

Crisp on the outside and moist and creamy on the inside, this traditional potato casserole is enlivened with chopped fresh parsley and thyme.

ACTIVE TIME: 25 MINUTES   **TOTAL TIME:** 1 HOUR 35 MINUTES
MAKES: 8 SIDE-DISH SERVINGS

4   tablespoons olive oil

1   large onion (10 to 12 ounces), finely chopped

3   large eggs

1   large egg white

¼   cup packed fresh flat-leaf parsley leaves, finely chopped

1   teaspoon salt

¼   teaspoon ground black pepper

1   teaspoon fresh thyme leaves, chopped, plus sprigs for garnish

3   pounds all-purpose potatoes

1 Preheat oven to 400°F. Brush shallow 2-quart ceramic or glass baking dish with 1 tablespoon oil.
2 In 12-inch skillet, heat 1 tablespoon oil over medium heat until hot. Add onion and cook, stirring occasionally, until golden brown and tender, about 9 minutes. Meanwhile, in large bowl, with whisk, beat eggs, egg white, parsley, salt, and pepper until blended. Add thyme to skillet and cook, stirring occasionally, 1 minute. Remove skillet from heat.

3 Working quickly, peel potatoes and grate in food processor with grating attachment or on the large holes of a box grater. Add potatoes to egg mixture as you grate to prevent potatoes from turning gray; then add onions. Stir until well blended. Transfer potato mixture to prepared baking dish and spread in even layer. Brush top of potatoes with remaining 2 tablespoons oil.
4 Bake until browned on top and tip of small sharp knife pierces easily through potato mixture, 1 hour to 1 hour 10 minutes. Let stand 10 to 15 minutes for easier serving. Garnish with thyme sprigs; serve warm.

EACH SERVING: ABOUT 210 CALORIES, 6G PROTEIN, 28G CARBOHYDRATE, 9G TOTAL FAT (2G SATURATED), 3G FIBER, 80MG CHOLESTEROL, 330MG SODIUM.

TIP

To make ahead, cool completely, cover with foil, and refrigerate up to overnight. Reheat, covered, in 400°F oven 30 minutes or until warm.

SWEET POTATOES WITH
Marshmallow Meringue

To update this holiday classic, we zapped
the potatoes before mashing and topped them
with meringue mounds—a less-sugary substitute
for typical mini marshmallows.

ACTIVE TIME: 30 MINUTES **TOTAL TIME:** 50 MINUTES
MAKES: 12 SIDE-DISH SERVINGS

3   pounds sweet potatoes

2   tablespoons pure maple syrup

1   tablespoon dark brown sugar

1   tablespoon fresh lemon juice

3/4 teaspoon salt

1/8 teaspoon ground allspice

3   large egg whites

1/4 teaspoon cream of tartar

1/3 cup granulated sugar

1 Preheat oven to 400°F. Pierce sweet potatoes all over with tip of knife; place in large microwave-safe bowl. Cover with vented plastic wrap and microwave on High until very tender when pierced with fork, 15 to 17 minutes; drain. When cool enough to handle, peel potatoes and return to bowl.

2 To bowl with sweet potatoes, add maple syrup, brown sugar, lemon juice, salt, and allspice. Mash potatoes with potato masher until smooth. Transfer mashed potatoes to shallow 2-quart baking dish. (If making ahead, cover and refrigerate up to overnight; uncover and bake in 400°F oven until heated through, about 15 minutes.)

3 **Prepare Meringue:** In large bowl, with mixer on high speed, beat egg whites and cream of tartar until soft peaks form. Sprinkle in granulated sugar, 2 tablespoons at a time, beating until sugar dissolves and meringue stands in stiff, glossy peaks when beaters are lifted.

4 Transfer meringue to large piping bag fitted with 1/2-inch plain tip or to heavy-duty gallon-size zip-tight plastic bag with one corner cut to form 1/2-inch hole. Starting at one side of baking dish, pipe meringue in small mounds onto surface of sweet potatoes, covering entire surface. Bake until meringue is golden, 6 to 8 minutes.

EACH SERVING: ABOUT 100 CALORIES, 2G PROTEIN, 23G CARBOHYDRATE, 0G TOTAL FAT (0G SATURATED), 7G FIBER, 0MG CHOLESTEROL, 183MG SODIUM.

Italian Spiced Shrimp
(page 100)

5 Party Perfect

Expecting guests? Leave nothing to chance, so wow the crowd with one of these easy-bake casseroles. Choose from all-American faves like King Ranch Chicken (page 89) or Macaroni & Cheese Deluxe (page 97). If you want to make a splash—and take the guesswork out of cooking fish—our "shore"-fire specials like Lentils & Cod (page 103) or Seafood Stuffed Shells (page 104) are guaranteed to reel in rave reviews. Or if your crew is meat-and-potatoes only, our take on shepherd's pie is a knock-out.

Best of all, these entertaining lifesavers can be assembled ahead; simply cover and refrigerate up to 24 hours. To serve, let the casserole stand at room temperature 1 hour, bake as directed, then enjoy a bubbling masterpiece with friends. Now *that's* a smart party plan!

KING RANCH **Chicken**

This popular Tex-Mex casserole got its name from one of the largest ranches in Texas. Cheesy meets spicy, with poblano and jalapeño chiles providing a double dose of heat.

ACTIVE TIME: 30 MINUTES   **TOTAL TIME:** 1 HOUR
MAKES: 6 MAIN-DISH SERVINGS

2   cups low-fat (1%) milk

2   tablespoons vegetable oil

1   small onion (4 to 6 ounces), finely chopped

1   large red pepper (8 to 10 ounces), finely chopped

1   large poblano chile (4 to 6 ounces), seeds discarded, finely chopped

1   jalapeño chile, seeds discarded, finely chopped

2   cloves garlic, crushed with garlic press

3   tablespoons all-purpose flour

1   cup reduced-sodium chicken broth

1   can (14½ ounces) no-salt-added diced tomatoes, drained

¼   teaspoon salt

¼   teaspoon ground black pepper

3½ ounces baked tortilla chips, crushed (about 1¼ cups)

2   cups cooked, shredded chicken breast meat

4   ounces pepper Jack or Monterey Jack cheese, shredded (2 cups)

1   green onion, thinly sliced, for garnish

1 Preheat oven to 350°F. Grease shallow 3-quart ceramic or glass baking dish. In 2-cup glass measuring cup, microwave milk on High until warm, 2 minutes.

2 Meanwhile, in 12-inch skillet, heat oil over medium-high heat until hot. Add onion, red pepper, poblano chile, and jalapeño chile. Cook, stirring occasionally, until vegetables are just tender, about 4 minutes. Add garlic and cook, stirring, 1 minute.

3 Add flour and cook, stirring, 1 minute. Continue stirring and add broth, then milk, in steady stream. Heat to boiling while stirring, then cook, stirring constantly, until thickened, about 3 minutes. Stir in tomatoes, salt, and black pepper.

4 Spread thin, even layer of sauce on bottom of prepared baking dish. Top with half of chips, sauce, chicken, and cheese. Repeat layering once. Bake until bubbly, about 30 minutes. Garnish with green onions.

EACH SERVING: ABOUT 365 CALORIES, 22G PROTEIN, 30G CARBOHYDRATE, 18G TOTAL FAT (6G SATURATED), 3G FIBER, 60MG CHOLESTEROL, 535MG SODIUM.

TIP
Try this dish with cooked shredded turkey breast.

LAYERED LAMB &
Potato Casserole

Browned ground lamb simmers in a cinnamon-scented tomato sauce with fresh chopped mint, and is then layered with thinly sliced potatoes and a creamy yogurt-and-feta sauce.

ACTIVE TIME: 45 MINUTES   **TOTAL TIME:** 1 HOUR 35 MINUTES
MAKES: 6 MAIN-DISH SERVINGS

5   medium red potatoes (about 1½ pounds)

1½ pounds ground lamb or ground beef chuck

1   tablespoon olive oil

3   cloves garlic, crushed with garlic press

1   large onion, chopped

½   teaspoon ground cinnamon

¼   cup tomato paste

1   teaspoon salt

¼   teaspoon ground black pepper

1   can (14 to 14½ ounces) chicken broth (1¾ cups)

1   cup loosely packed fresh mint leaves, chopped

2   large eggs

1½ cups low-fat plain yogurt

8   ounces feta cheese, crumbled (2 cups)

2   tablespoons cornstarch

1 In microwave-safe small bowl, combine unpeeled potatoes and *2 tablespoons water*. Cover with vented plastic wrap and microwave on High 5 minutes or just until fork-tender but not soft, stirring potatoes once. Remove plastic wrap from bowl; cool potatoes slightly.

2 Meanwhile, heat 12-inch nonstick skillet over medium heat. Add lamb and cook, stirring to break it up with side of spoon, until browned, about 8 minutes. With slotted spoon, transfer lamb to medium bowl. Wipe skillet clean.

3 In same skillet, heat oil over medium heat until hot. Add garlic, onion, and cinnamon and cook, stirring, until tender, 6 to 7 minutes. Return lamb to skillet; stir in tomato paste, salt, pepper, and 1 cup broth. Heat to boiling; cook 5 minutes. Remove skillet from heat; stir in mint.

4 Meanwhile, preheat oven to 375°F. In medium bowl, with fork, mix eggs, yogurt, feta, cornstarch, and remaining ¾ cup broth. Cut unpeeled potatoes into ⅛-inch-thick slices; discard cooking water.

5 Spoon about 1¼ cups yogurt mixture into bottom of ungreased 13" by 9" ceramic or glass baking dish. Top evenly with half of potatoes, overlapping slightly, then half of lamb mixture. Repeat layering with remaining potatoes and lamb mixture, ending with potatoes. Spoon remaining yogurt mixture on top.

6 Bake until top browns, about 45 minutes. Let stand 10 minutes for easier serving.

EACH SERVING: ABOUT 570 CALORIES, 36G PROTEIN, 38G CARBOHYDRATE, 30G TOTAL FAT (14G SATURATED), 4G FIBER, 190MG CHOLESTEROL, 1,250MG SODIUM.

SWEET POTATO
Shepherd's Pie

Fluffy sweet potatoes stand in
for the usual spuds atop a turkey filling
with collard greens and Cajun seasoning.

ACTIVE TIME: 30 MINUTES **TOTAL TIME:** 1 HOUR 10 MINUTES
MAKES: 6 MAIN-DISH SERVINGS

2½ pounds sweet potatoes

½ cup low-fat (1%) milk

salt

¼ teaspoon ground black pepper

1 tablespoon plus 1 teaspoon vegetable oil

1 large onion, finely chopped

1 bunch collard greens (12 ounces), stems
   discarded, leaves very thinly sliced

2 cloves garlic, chopped

1 pound lean (93%) ground turkey

2 teaspoons salt-free Cajun seasoning

2 tablespoons tomato paste

1 tablespoon finely chopped flat-leaf parsley
   leaves, for garnish

1 Preheat oven to 400°F.

2 In large microwave-safe bowl, combine sweet
potatoes and ¼ cup water. Cover with vented
plastic wrap and microwave on High 15 minutes
or until tender. When cool enough to handle,
discard peels. In large bowl, mash potatoes with
milk, ⅛ teaspoon salt, and ⅛ teaspoon pepper.

3 Meanwhile, in 12-inch skillet, heat 1 tablespoon
oil over medium-high heat until hot. Add onion
and cook, stirring occasionally, until browned,
about 5 minutes. Add collard greens, ⅛ teaspoon
salt, and remaining ⅛ teaspoon pepper. Cook,
stirring, until just wilted, about 1 minute. Transfer
to medium bowl.

4 In same skillet, heat remaining 1 teaspoon oil.
Add garlic and cook 15 seconds. Add turkey and
¼ teaspoon salt. Cook, stirring and breaking up
turkey with side of spoon, until browned, about
3 minutes. Reduce heat to medium and add Cajun
seasoning. Cook, stirring, 1 minute. Add tomato
paste and ¼ cup water. Cook, stirring, 2 minutes.

5 In 8" by 8" shallow ceramic or glass baking
dish, spread half of mashed sweet potatoes in an
even layer. Top evenly with turkey mixture, then
collard greens mixture. Spread remaining sweet
potato mixture evenly on top. Bake until golden
on top, about 30 minutes. Garnish with parsley.

EACH SERVING: ABOUT 290 CALORIES, 19G PROTEIN,
36G CARBOHYDRATE, 9G TOTAL FAT (2G SATURATED),
7G FIBER, 44MG CHOLESTEROL, 350MG SODIUM.

CREOLE "Cassoulet"

Spicy Andouille sausage stars in our jazzy take on
the renowned bean casserole from France.
You can also substitute kielbasa sausage, but add a good pinch
of crushed red pepper to the mix.

ACTIVE TIME: 20 MINUTES   TOTAL TIME: 2 HOURS 40 MINUTES PLUS STANDING
MAKES: 8 MAIN-DISH SERVINGS

1   pound dried red kidney beans

1   head garlic, peeled and finely chopped
    (about 15 cloves)

3   green onions, finely chopped

3   stalks celery, chopped

1   medium onion, chopped

1   small green pepper, chopped

½   pound good-quality smoked bacon, very
    thinly sliced crosswise

1½ pounds Andouille sausage, sliced on an angle

4   tablespoons butter or margarine

¾   cup panko (Japanese-style breadcrumbs)

Creole or Dijon mustard, for serving

1 In 5- or 6-quart heavy-bottomed saucepot or Dutch oven, combine beans and *6 cups water*. Let stand 1 hour.

2 Drain soaking liquid from beans; add *6 cups cold water*. Heat to boiling over medium-high heat. Stir in garlic, green onions, celery, onion, and green pepper. Heat to simmering. Reduce heat to low. Gently simmer, uncovered, until beans are very tender, about 2 hours.

3 Meanwhile, preheat oven to 400°F. Arrange bacon in single layer on rimmed baking sheet. Roast, stirring every 5 minutes, until crispy, about 15 minutes. Transfer bacon to pot with beans. Discard fat from baking sheet. To same sheet, add sausage. Roast, stirring twice, until crisp around edges, about 20 minutes. Add sausage to beans; continue cooking. (If mixture begins to dry out, stir in up to *½ cup water*.)

4 Reset oven to 350°F. When beans are cooked, transfer to shallow 3-quart baking dish. In 8-inch skillet, melt butter over medium heat. Add panko. Cook, stirring, until golden brown, about 3 minutes. Spoon crumbs evenly over bean mixture. Bake 35 minutes. Serve with mustard.

EACH SERVING: ABOUT 490 CALORIES, 32G PROTEIN, 43G CARBOHYDRATE, 22G TOTAL FAT (10G SATURATED), 11G FIBER, 76MG CHOLESTEROL, 860MG SODIUM.

PARTY PERFECT

MACARONI & CHEESE
Deluxe

Hello decadence! This sophisticated bake
features blue cheese, sweet pear-shaped tomatoes,
and toasted walnuts.

ACTIVE TIME: 30 MINUTES **TOTAL TIME:** 55 MINUTES
MAKES: 6 MAIN-DISH SERVINGS

1	package (16 ounces) penne
3	tablespoons butter or margarine
1	medium onion, diced
2	tablespoons all-purpose flour
¼	teaspoon salt
¼	teaspoon coarsely ground black pepper
¼	teaspoon cayenne (ground red) pepper
¼	teaspoon ground nutmeg
4	cups low-fat (1%) milk
½	cup freshly grated Parmesan cheese
1	cup frozen peas
4	ounces creamy blue cheese (like Gorgonzola), cut up or crumbled into pieces (1 cup)
½	pint pear-shaped or round cherry tomatoes, cut in half
½	cup walnuts, toasted

1 Heat large covered saucepot of *salted water* to boiling over high heat. Add pasta and cook as label directs. Preheat oven to 400°F.

2 Meanwhile, in shallow 3-quart saucepan, melt butter over medium heat. Add onion and cook, stirring occasionally, until tender, 8 to 10 minutes. With whisk, stir in flour, salt, black pepper, cayenne pepper, and nutmeg, and cook, stirring constantly, 1 minute. Slowly whisk in milk and cook over medium-high heat, stirring frequently, until sauce boils and thickens slightly. Boil 1 minute, stirring. Stir in ¼ cup Parmesan. Remove saucepan from heat.

3 Place frozen peas in colander; drain pasta over peas and return pasta mixture to saucepot. Stir in sauce and blue cheese. Transfer pasta mixture to deep 3-quart baking dish.

4 In small bowl, toss tomatoes with remaining ¼ cup Parmesan. Top casserole with tomatoes. Bake until hot and bubbly and top is lightly browned, about 20 minutes. Sprinkle with walnuts.

....

EACH SERVING: ABOUT 610 CALORIES, 26G PROTEIN, 76G CARBOHYDRATE, 23G TOTAL FAT (6G SATURATED), 5G FIBER, 43MG CHOLESTEROL, 965MG SODIUM.

PARTY PERFECT

TEX MEX **Lasagna**

Oven-ready lasagna noodles are an easy stand-in
for the usual fried tortillas in this easy bake layered with
veggies, refried beans, salsa, and cheese.

ACTIVE TIME: 20 MINUTES **TOTAL TIME:** 1 HOUR 15 MINUTES
MAKES: 6 MAIN-DISH SERVINGS

2 teaspoons vegetable oil

1 small onion (4 to 6 ounces), chopped

2 medium zucchini, thinly sliced

1 jar (16 ounces) salsa

1 cup fresh or frozen (thawed) corn

1 tablespoon no-salt-added chili powder

1 can (8 ounces) tomato sauce

6 oven-ready (no-boil) lasagna noodles

1 can (16 ounces) fat-free refried beans

8 ounces Monterey Jack or cheddar cheese,
   shredded (2 cups)

½ cup packed fresh cilantro leaves

1 Preheat oven to 400°F. Spray shallow 2-quart
baking dish with nonstick cooking spray.
2 In 12-inch skillet, heat oil over medium-
high heat until hot. Add onion. Cook, stirring
occasionally, until beginning to soften, about
2 minutes. Stir in zucchini, salsa, corn, and
chili powder. Cook, stirring occasionally, until
zucchini is crisp-tender, 2 to 3 minutes. Remove
skillet from heat.
3 On bottom of prepared baking dish, spread
half of tomato sauce. Arrange 2 lasagna noodles
in single layer. Top evenly with half of beans
and half of vegetables. Arrange 2 more lasagna
noodles in single layer. Top evenly with half of
cheese. Repeat with remaining sauce, noodles,
beans, and vegetables. Top evenly with remaining
cheese.
4 Cover tightly with foil and bake 30 minutes.
Remove foil and bake until bubbly and noodles
are tender, 15 to 20 minutes longer. Let stand
5 minutes for easier serving. Top with cilantro.

EACH SERVING: ABOUT 365 CALORIES, 18G PROTEIN,
41G CARBOHYDRATE, 15G TOTAL FAT (8G SATURATED),
7G FIBER, 34MG CHOLESTEROL, 960MG SODIUM.

Casserole + Salad = Party

A knockout casserole and a big salad are all you need
for a well-planned dinner. Here are three exceptional combos:

MEDITERRANEAN FEAST

Layered Lamb & Potato Casserole (page 90) + cucumber,
tomato, and red onion salad with lemon-dill dressing.

FIESTA SUPPER

King Ranch Chicken (page 89) + red and
green slaw with shredded jicama and buttermilk-
chive dressing.

ELEGANT DINNER

Seafood Stuffed Shells (page 104) + arugula,
frisée, and radicchio salad with
balsamic vinaigrette.

LOOKING FOR DESSERT?

That's easy! Grab another baking dish and try these do-ahead treats
(they go with any of our menus): Spiced Chocolate Bread Pudding (page 123),
Deep-Dish Apple Cobbler (page 121), or Bumbleberry Crisp (page 111).

PARTY PERFECT

ITALIAN SPICED
Shrimp

A zesty mix of shrimp with tomatoes, white wine,
and crushed red pepper baked atop an herbed rice pilaf
makes this fabulous party fare one-dish easy.
For photo, see page 86.

ACTIVE TIME: 20 MINUTES **TOTAL TIME:** 40 MINUTES
MAKES: 4 MAIN-DISH SERVINGS

1   small onion (4 to 6 ounces)

1   tablespoon fresh oregano leaves

1   cup long-grain white rice

1   tablespoon olive oil

¼ to ½ teaspoon crushed red pepper, to taste

2   cloves garlic, crushed with garlic press

1   cup dry white wine

1   can (28 ounces) no-salt-added diced
    tomatoes, drained well

½   teaspoon salt

½   teaspoon ground black pepper

1   pound large shrimp, shelled and deveined,
    with tail part of shell left on if you like

8   fresh basil leaves, very thinly sliced,
    for garnish

1 Preheat oven to 400°F. While oven heats, finely chop onion and oregano.

2 In shallow 3-quart baking dish, combine rice and *1¾ cups hot water*. Cover tightly with foil and bake until rice is tender and all liquid is absorbed, about 20 minutes.

3 Meanwhile, in 5- to 6-quart saucepot, heat oil over medium heat until hot. Add onion, oregano, and crushed red pepper; cook, stirring occasionally, 3 minutes. Add garlic and cook, stirring, until golden, about 30 seconds. Add wine and heat to boiling; reduce heat to medium-low and simmer, stirring occasionally, until wine is reduced by half, about 6 minutes. Stir in tomatoes, salt, and black pepper. Remove saucepot from heat.

4 Remove baking dish from oven. Arrange shrimp on top of rice in baking dish in single layer. Pour tomato mixture evenly over shrimp; cover baking dish tightly with foil and bake until shrimp turn opaque, about 15 minutes longer. Garnish with basil.

EACH SERVING: ABOUT 370 CALORIES, 24G PROTEIN, 52G CARBOHYDRATE, 6G TOTAL FAT (1G SATURATED), 3G FIBER, 140MG CHOLESTEROL, 450MG SODIUM.

LOUISIANA SEAFOOD
Casserole

While the trio of seafood—monkfish, scallops,
and shrimp—qualifies this casserole as special occasion,
the other ingredients, like parboiled rice and stewed
tomatoes, mean it's pantry-friendly too.

ACTIVE TIME: 30 MINUTES   **TOTAL TIME:** 1 HOUR 20 MINUTES
MAKES: 6 MAIN-DISH SERVINGS

3/4   pound hot Italian sausage links

2   medium celery stalks, cut into ½-inch pieces

1   large red pepper, cut into ½-inch pieces

1   large green pepper, cut into ½-inch pieces

1   medium onion, diced

1   package (16 ounces) parboiled rice

2   cans (14 to 14½ ounces each) chicken broth

1   can (14½ to 16 ounces) stewed tomatoes

1   bay leaf

½   teaspoon hot pepper sauce

¼   teaspoon dried thyme

1   pound monkfish or scrod fillets

3/4   pound large shrimp

3/4   pound sea scallops

2   tablespoons chopped fresh parsley

1 Preheat oven to 350°F. In 8-quart Dutch
oven, cook sausage over medium-high heat until
browned; with slotted spoon, transfer sausage to
paper towels to drain.

2 In drippings in Dutch oven, cook celery, red and
green peppers, and onion, stirring occasionally,
until tender and golden. Meanwhile, cut cooked
sausages into ½-inch-thick diagonal slices.

3 Add rice to vegetables and cook, stirring, until
rice is opaque. Stir in broth, tomatoes, bay leaf,
pepper sauce, thyme, and sausage; heat to boiling
over high heat. Cover and bake 25 minutes.

4 Meanwhile, pull tough, grayish membrane
from monkfish fillets, and cut monkfish into
1½-inch pieces. Shell and devein shrimp. Pull
tough muscle from side of each scallop. Rinse
shellfish with cold running water.

5 Stir monkfish, shrimp, and scallops into rice
mixture. Cover and bake, stirring occasionally,
until rice is tender and seafood is opaque
throughout, 20 to 25 minutes longer. Discard
bay leaf. Stir in parsley.

EACH SERVING: ABOUT 500 CALORIES, 37G PROTEIN,
56G CARBOHYDRATE, 13G TOTAL FAT (4G SATURATED),
4G FIBER, 127MG CHOLESTEROL, 720MG SODIUM.

LENTILS & Cod

Herbes de Provence—a savory mixture of
dried lavender, marjoram, rosemary, sage, basil, and
fennel seeds—adds a uniquely aromatic touch
to this elegant casserole.

ACTIVE TIME: 40 MINUTES   **TOTAL TIME:** 1 HOUR 5 MINUTES
MAKES: 6 MAIN-DISH SERVINGS

1   tablespoon olive oil

2   medium carrots, diced

1   medium onion, diced

1   large celery stalk, diced

½   teaspoon herbes de Provence

¼   teaspoon fennel seeds

3   strips orange peel (3" by 1" each)

3   cloves garlic, crushed with garlic press

8   ounces dried lentils (1 cup), rinsed
     and picked over

1   can (14 to 14½ ounces) reduced-sodium
     chicken broth (1¾ cups)

¾   teaspoon salt

½   teaspoon coarsely ground black pepper

1   can (14½ ounces) whole tomatoes in puree

4   pieces cod fillet (6 ounces each)

thyme sprigs and thinly sliced orange peel,
     for garnish

1 In 4-quart saucepan, heat oil over medium-high heat until hot. Add carrots, onion, and celery, and cook, stirring occasionally, until lightly browned, about 10 minutes.

2 Add herbes de Provence, fennel seeds, orange peel, and garlic; cook, stirring, 2 minutes.

3 Add lentils, broth, and *2 cups water*; heat to boiling over high heat. Reduce heat to low; cover and simmer, stirring occasionally, 20 minutes. Add ½ teaspoon salt, ¼ teaspoon pepper, and tomatoes with their puree, stirring and breaking up tomatoes with side of spoon. Heat to boiling over high heat. Reduce heat to low; cover and simmer 5 minutes.

4 Preheat oven to 400°F. Transfer lentil mixture to shallow 2½-quart baking dish. Place cod fillets on top of lentil mixture; sprinkle cod with remaining ¼ teaspoon salt and remaining ¼ teaspoon pepper. Cover baking dish with foil and bake until fish flakes easily when tested with fork and lentils are tender, 20 to 25 minutes. Discard cooked orange peel. Garnish with thyme sprigs and sliced orange-peel.

EACH SERVING: ABOUT 325 CALORIES, 32G PROTEIN, 40G CARBOHYDRATE, 4G TOTAL FAT (1G SATURATED), 8G FIBER, 49MG CHOLESTEROL, 760MG SODIUM.

TIP

If you can't find herbes de Provence, substitute ¼ teaspoon dried thyme and ¼ teaspoon dried rosemary, crushed, and increase fennel seeds to ½ teaspoon.

SEAFOOD **Stuffed Shells**

Instead of typical cheese-filled shells, impress guests with this savory filling of shrimp and scrod with a creamy tomato sauce.

ACTIVE TIME: 1 HOUR 15 MINUTES **TOTAL TIME:** 1 HOUR 35 MINUTES
MAKES: 10 MAIN-DISH SERVINGS

30 jumbo pasta shells

salt

1 tablespoon olive oil

1 small onion, chopped

2 cloves garlic, minced

1 bottle (8 ounces) clam juice

1 can (28 ounces) whole tomatoes in puree

2 tablespoons tomato paste

1 teaspoon sugar

1/4 teaspoon crushed red pepper

1/3 cup heavy or whipping cream

1 pound medium shrimp, shelled, deveined, and coarsely chopped

1 pound scrod fillet, coarsely chopped

1 package (10 ounces) frozen peas

BREADCRUMB TOPPING

1 tablespoon olive oil

1 clove garlic, crushed with side of chef's knife

2 slices firm white bread, torn into 1/4-inch pieces

1 Cook pasta shells in *boiling salted water* as label directs. Drain shells and rinse with cold running water to stop cooking; drain again. Arrange shells in single layer on waxed paper and set aside.

2 Meanwhile, in 4-quart saucepan, heat oil over medium heat until hot. Add onion and cook, stirring, until softened, about 4 minutes. Add garlic and cook, stirring frequently, 1 minute. Add clam juice and cook over high heat until reduced to 1/2 cup, about 7 minutes. Stir in tomatoes with their puree, breaking up tomatoes with side of spoon. Add tomato paste, sugar, and crushed red pepper; heat to boiling over high heat. Reduce heat to low; partially cover and simmer, stirring occasionally, 20 minutes. Stir in cream and cook 2 minutes; remove saucepan from heat.

3 Transfer 1 cup tomato sauce to 3-quart saucepan. Add shrimp and scrod. Cook, stirring occasionally, over medium-high heat until seafood turns opaque throughout, about 5 minutes. Remove saucepan from heat; stir equal amounts frozen peas into both saucepans.

4 Preheat oven to 400°F. Fill each pasta shell with 2 heaping tablespoons seafood mixture and place in 13" by 9" glass baking dish. Pour tomato sauce over stuffed shells.

5 **Prepare Breadcrumb Topping:** In 10-inch nonstick skillet, heat oil and garlic over medium heat until hot. Add breadcrumbs and cook, stirring frequently, until golden, about 5 minutes. Discard garlic.

6 Spoon breadcrumbs over stuffed shells. Bake until hot and bubbly, about 20 minutes.

....

EACH SERVING: ABOUT 325 CALORIES, 23G PROTEIN, 38G CARBOHYDRATE, 9G TOTAL FAT (3G SATURATED), 5G FIBER, 87MG CHOLESTEROL, 450MG SODIUM.

Peach-Raspberry Crisp
(page 112)

6 Sweet & Bubbly

Take your favorite fruit, toss it in a baking dish with something sweet, add a topping, and what do you have? Comfort dessert at its best. This collection of crisps and cobblers (aka "spoon pies" that require only a bowl and spoon to enjoy) are distinguished by their single upper crust and luscious double-the-fruit filling. Choices like our summery Bumbleberry Crisp (page 111), Peach & Blueberry Crumble (page 113) and Deep-Dish Apple Cobbler (page 121), need only a scoop of ice cream or dollop of whipped cream to qualify as sweet bliss.

And, like savory casseroles, sweet ones are just as easy to make—a simple toss of butter, flour, sugar, and spices are all that's required for a streusel-like crisp topping. Even our splashy Spiced Chocolate Bread Pudding (page 123) is tailor-made for the beginner baker. That makes lovin' from the oven a very sweet event indeed.

EASY PLUM
Crumble

Juicy, sweet-tart plums are ideal for baked desserts.
From May until late October, you'll find them
in a rainbow of colors from deep purple
to red and yellow.

ACTIVE TIME: 20 MINUTES   **TOTAL TIME:** 50 MINUTES
MAKES: 6 SERVINGS

2½ pounds plums, pitted and cut into
   8 wedges

1   tablespoon fresh lemon juice

⅔ cup packed light brown sugar

1   tablespoon cornstarch

1   cup old-fashioned oats, uncooked

⅓ cup all-purpose flour

½   teaspoon ground cinnamon

4   tablespoons cold butter or margarine,
   cut into pieces

1 Preheat oven to 400°F. In shallow 2-quart glass or ceramic baking dish, toss plums with lemon juice. In cup, mix ⅓ cup brown sugar and cornstarch; toss with plums until evenly coated.
2 In medium bowl, mix remaining ⅓ cup brown sugar with oats, flour, and cinnamon. With fingertips, work in butter until mixture resembles coarse crumbs. Sprinkle oat topping over plum mixture.
3 Bake until plums are tender and topping is lightly browned, 25 to 30 minutes. Cool on wire rack about 10 minutes to serve warm, or cool completely to serve later. Reheat if desired.

EACH SERVING: ABOUT 340 CALORIES, 4G PROTEIN, 63G CARBOHYDRATE, 10G TOTAL FAT (5G SATURATED), 4G FIBER, 22MG CHOLESTEROL, 95MG SODIUM.

TIP

Select firm-ripe plums for baking. Take a plum and squeeze it gently in the palm of your hand. It should smell fragrant and feel firm yet springy.

BUMBLEBERRY
Crisp

Three kinds of berries—plus sweet Golden Delicious apples—
are topped with a heavenly hazelnut streusel.

ACTIVE TIME: 15 MINUTES   **TOTAL TIME:** 1 HOUR PLUS STANDING
MAKES: 6 SERVINGS

1   cup hazelnuts (filberts), toasted
    (see Tip, below)

1   cup all-purpose flour

1/3   cup firmly packed light brown sugar

1/4   teaspoon ground cinnamon

1/4   teaspoon salt

6   tablespoons cold butter or margarine,
    cut into pieces

2   Golden Delicious apples, cored, peeled,
    and chopped

1   pound strawberries, hulled and sliced
    (about 3 cups)

1   container (6 ounces) blueberries

1   container (6 ounces) raspberries

3/4   cup granulated sugar

1/4   cup cornstarch

3   tablespoons fresh lemon juice

vanilla ice cream, optional

1 Preheat oven to 375°F. Grease shallow 2-quart baking dish.

2 Chop hazelnuts. In medium bowl, mix flour, brown sugar, cinnamon, and salt. With fingertips, work in butter until small clumps form. Stir in hazelnuts.

3 In large bowl, combine apples, strawberries, blueberries, raspberries, granulated sugar, cornstarch, and lemon juice until evenly coated; transfer to prepared baking dish. Sprinkle nut mixture evenly on top. Bake until bubbly and golden, about 45 minutes. Let cool on wire rack about 30 minutes to serve warm. Serve with ice cream, if using.

EACH SERVING: ABOUT 560 CALORIES, 7G PROTEIN, 81G CARBOHYDRATE, 26G TOTAL FAT (8G SATURATED), 7G FIBER, 31MG CHOLESTEROL, 205MG SODIUM.

TIP

To toast hazelnuts, spread them in an 8" by 8" metal baking pan. Bake the nuts at 375°F, shaking the pan occasionally, until fragrant, about 8 minutes. Remove the pan from the oven. Wrap the hot nuts in a clean cloth towel; with your hands, roll the nuts back and forth until as much skin as possible rubs off. Cool the nuts completely.

PEACH-RASPBERRY
Crisp

Super-sweet summer peaches and raspberries
are crowned with an extra-crisp crumb topping.
The secret to the topping? Demerara sugar: coarse,
golden crystals with a wonderful caramel taste.

ACTIVE TIME: 35 MINUTES   **TOTAL TIME:** 1 HOUR 35 MINUTES PLUS STANDING
MAKES: 8 SERVINGS

- 1   large lemon
- 1⅓ cups all-purpose flour
- 1   teaspoon baking powder
- 3   tablespoons Demerara or light brown sugar
- ½   cup plus 3 tablespoons granulated sugar
- 10 tablespoons unsalted butter, melted
- 6   ripe peaches, peeled and halved
- 1   pint raspberries
- ¼   cup cornstarch
- ⅛   teaspoon salt
- whipped cream or vanilla ice cream, optional

1 From lemon, grate 1 tablespoon peel; squeeze 3 tablespoons juice. In large bowl, combine flour, baking powder, Demerara sugar, 3 tablespoons granulated sugar, and lemon peel; blend in melted butter until small and large clumps form. Refrigerate 15 minutes.

2 Preheat oven to 375°F.

3 Cut peaches into ¼-inch-thick slices. In bowl, toss peaches, raspberries, cornstarch, salt, lemon juice, and remaining ½ cup granulated sugar until evenly coated. Let stand 15 minutes.

4 In shallow 2-quart ceramic baking dish, spread fruit in an even layer. Top evenly with crumbs. Bake until filling is bubbly, 40 to 50 minutes. Let cool on wire rack about 30 minutes to serve warm. Serve with whipped cream or ice cream, if using.

....

EACH SERVING: ABOUT 365 CALORIES, 4G PROTEIN, 56G CARBOHYDRATE, 15G TOTAL FAT (9G SATURATED), 4G FIBER, 38MG CHOLESTEROL, 85MG SODIUM.

TIP

To remove tough skins from fresh peaches, submerge them in boiling water for 15 to 20 seconds. With a slotted spoon, immediately transfer the fruit to a bowl of ice water. When cool enough to handle, drain and peel. The skins should slip right off.

PEACH & BLUEBERRY
Crumble

This peachy-keen dessert is also terrific
if you sub in blackberries. A combo of butter and
canola oil gives the topping extra crunch.

ACTIVE TIME: 20 MINUTES   **TOTAL TIME:** 55 MINUTES
MAKES: 8 SERVINGS

¼ cup hazelnuts (filberts), toasted
(see Tip, page 111)

2½ pounds ripe peaches, peeled, pitted, and
sliced

1 pint blueberries (about 2½ cups)

½ cup packed light brown sugar

⅓ cup all-purpose flour

1 cup old-fashioned oats, uncooked

1 teaspoon ground cinnamon

2 tablespoons cold butter or margarine,
cut into pieces

2 tablespoons canola oil

1 Preheat oven to 400°F.

2 In shallow 2-quart ceramic or glass baking
dish, toss peaches, blueberries, ¼ cup brown
sugar, and 1 tablespoon flour until evenly coated.
Spread fruit mixture in an even layer in baking
dish.

3 In medium bowl, mix oats, cinnamon,
remaining flour, and remaining ¼ cup brown
sugar. Add butter and oil. With fingertips, blend
until mixture resembles coarse crumbs. Mix in
hazelnuts. Sprinkle topping evenly over fruit.

4 Bake until fruit is bubbly at edges and topping
is browned, 30 to 35 minutes. Cover loosely
with foil after 25 minutes if top is browning too
quickly. Cool slightly on wire rack to serve warm,
or serve at room temperature.

EACH SERVING: ABOUT 270 CALORIES, 4G PROTEIN,
45G CARBOHYDRATE, 10G TOTAL FAT (1G SATURATED),
5G FIBER, 8MG CHOLESTEROL, 45MG SODIUM.

APPLE-OAT
Crisp

This crisp is terrific with either tart Granny Smith
or sweeter Golden Delicious apples,
as both hold their shape well when baked.
Or try a combination of the two.

ACTIVE TIME: 15 MINUTES **TOTAL TIME:** 45 MINUTES
MAKES: 12 SERVINGS

1 lemon

3 pounds Granny Smith and/or Golden Delicious apples, cored, peeled, and cut into 1-inch wedges

⅓ cup plus ¼ cup packed light brown sugar

2 tablespoons plus ⅓ cup all-purpose flour

1 teaspoon ground cinnamon

½ teaspoon salt

1 cup old-fashioned oats, uncooked

4 tablespoons butter or margarine, softened

vanilla yogurt, optional

1 Preheat oven to 425°F. From lemon, grate ½ teaspoon peel and squeeze 2 tablespoons juice. In 13" by 9" glass or ceramic baking dish, toss lemon peel and juice with apple wedges, ⅓ cup brown sugar, 2 tablespoons flour, cinnamon, and salt until apples are evenly coated.

2 In medium bowl, mix oats with remaining ¼ cup brown sugar and ⅓ cup flour. With fingertips, work in butter until mixture resembles coarse crumbs. Press crumb mixture into clumps and sprinkle evenly over apple mixture.

3 Bake until apples are tender and topping is lightly browned, 30 to 35 minutes. Cool on wire rack about 10 minutes to serve warm, or cool completely to serve later. Serve with yogurt, if using. Reheat if desired.

EACH SERVING: ABOUT 175 CALORIES, 2G PROTEIN, 33G CARBOHYDRATE, 5G TOTAL FAT (3G SATURATED), 3G FIBER, 11MG CHOLESTEROL, 145MG SODIUM.

TIP

Got leftover crisp? Cover the casserole with foil and refrigerate up to 1 day, then warm it, uncovered, in a 350°F oven.

SUGAR & SPICE
Blueberry Crisp

Here's summer's best: a true-blue bubbly fruit filling
topped with oats, brown sugar, and a hefty dose of cinnamon.

ACTIVE TIME: 20 MINUTES   **TOTAL TIME:** 55 MINUTES PLUS STANDING
MAKES: 8 SERVINGS

- ⅓ **cup granulated sugar**
- 2 **tablespoons cornstarch**
- 3 **pints blueberries**
- 1 **tablespoon fresh lemon juice**
- 1 **cup all-purpose flour**
- ¾ **cup quick-cooking or old-fashioned oats, uncooked**
- ⅓ **cup packed light brown sugar**
- ½ **cup (1 stick) cold butter or margarine, cut into pieces**
- ¾ **teaspoon ground cinnamon**

1 Preheat oven to 375°F. In large bowl, stir together granulated sugar and cornstarch until blended. Add blueberries and lemon juice; stir to coat evenly. Spoon blueberry mixture into shallow 2-quart glass or ceramic baking dish; spread evenly.

2 In same bowl, combine flour, oats, brown sugar, butter, and cinnamon. With fingertips, work in butter until mixture resembles coarse crumbs. Crumble evenly over blueberry mixture.

3 Place sheet of foil underneath baking dish; crimp foil edges to form a rim to catch any drips during baking. Bake until top is browned and fruit is bubbly at edges, 35 to 40 minutes. Cool on wire rack about 1 hour to serve warm, or cool completely to serve later.

EACH SERVING: ABOUT 390 CALORIES, 5G PROTEIN, 64G CARBOHYDRATE, 14G TOTAL FAT (8G SATURATED), 5G FIBER, 33MG CHOLESTEROL, 135MG SODIUM.

TIP

Quick-cooking and old-fashioned oats are interchangeable in crisp toppings. However, take a pass on instant oats, which are finely chopped and won't provide the same crunch factor you seek.

CHERRY-NECTARINE
Crisp

This sophisticated crisp combines nectarines,
sweet cherries, and a splash of brandy,
topped off with an oat-and-salted-almond streusel.

ACTIVE TIME: 30 MINUTES **TOTAL TIME:** 1 HOUR 15 MINUTES
MAKES: 8 SERVINGS

3 pounds nectarines, cut into wedges

1½ pounds cherries, pitted (3 cups)

¼ cup granulated sugar

3 tablespoons cornstarch

1 tablespoon fresh lemon juice

1 tablespoon brandy, optional

¾ cup packed light brown sugar

¾ cup old-fashioned oats, uncooked

⅓ cup all-purpose flour

½ cup roasted, salted almonds, chopped

¼ teaspoon freshly grated nutmeg

⅛ teaspoon salt

½ cup (1 stick) cold butter or margarine,
   cut up

1 Preheat oven to 375°F. Grease shallow 3-quart ceramic baking dish.

2 In large bowl, toss nectarines, cherries, granulated sugar, cornstarch, lemon juice, and brandy, if using, until well mixed. Spread in even layer in prepared baking dish.

3 In medium bowl, combine brown sugar, oats, flour, almonds, nutmeg, and salt. Add butter. With fingertips, work in butter until mixture resembles coarse crumbs. Sprinkle evenly over fruit mixture.

4 Bake until golden brown on top, 40 to 45 minutes. Cool slightly on wire rack to serve warm.

EACH SERVING: ABOUT 430 CALORIES, 6G PROTEIN, 69G CARBOHYDRATE, 17G TOTAL FAT (8G SATURATED), 6G FIBER, 31MG CHOLESTEROL, 175MG SODIUM.

TIP
For freshly grated nutmeg, protect your knuckles by using a rasp grater (versus the sharp perforated holes on a box grater).

RHUBARB-STRAWBERRY
Cobbler

Rhubarb makes this filling wonderfully
sweet and tart, but if you prefer it a little sweeter,
increase the sugar by ¼ cup.

ACTIVE TIME: 25 MINUTES **TOTAL TIME:** 45 MINUTES
MAKES: 8 SERVINGS

1¼ **pounds rhubarb, cut into 1-inch chunks (4 cups)**

¾ **cup plus 1 teaspoon sugar**

1 **tablespoon cornstarch**

1 **pint strawberries (¾ pound), hulled and cut into quarters**

1½ **cups all-purpose flour**

1½ **teaspoons baking powder**

½ **teaspoon baking soda**

¼ **teaspoon salt**

¼ **teaspoon ground cinnamon**

⅛ **teaspoon ground nutmeg**

4 **tablespoons cold butter or margarine, cut into pieces**

¾ **cup plus 1 tablespoon heavy or whipping cream**

¼ **teaspoon salt**

1 In 3-quart saucepan, heat rhubarb and ½ cup sugar to boiling over high heat, stirring constantly. Reduce heat to medium-low and cook until rhubarb is tender, about 8 minutes.

2 In cup, mix cornstarch with ¼ *cup water*. Stir cornstarch mixture and strawberries into rhubarb mixture; cook until mixture thickens slightly, about 2 minutes. Remove saucepan from heat.

3 Meanwhile, preheat oven to 400°F. In medium bowl, mix flour, baking powder, baking soda, salt, cinnamon, nutmeg, and ¼ cup sugar. With pastry blender or using 2 knives scissor-fashion, cut in butter until mixture resembles coarse crumbs. Add ¾ cup cream; quickly stir just until mixture forms a soft dough that pulls away from side of bowl.

4 Turn dough onto lightly floured surface; knead 6 to 8 strokes to mix thoroughly. With floured rolling pin, roll dough ½-inch thick. With floured 3-inch star-shaped cookie cutter, cut out as many biscuits as possible. Reroll trimmings and cut as above to make 8 biscuits in all.

5 Reheat rhubarb filling until hot; pour into shallow 2-quart casserole or 11" by 7" glass baking dish. Place biscuits on top of rhubarb. Brush biscuits with remaining 1 tablespoon cream and sprinkle with remaining 1 teaspoon sugar. Place sheet of foil under baking dish; crimp edges to form rim to catch any drips during baking. Bake until biscuits are golden brown and rhubarb filling is bubbly, about 20 minutes. Cool on wire rack about 15 minutes to serve warm.

EACH SERVING: ABOUT 375 CALORIES, 4G PROTEIN, 45G CARBOHYDRATE, 15G TOTAL FAT (7G SATURATED), 3G FIBER, 33MG CHOLESTEROL, 305MG SODIUM.

DEEP-DISH
Apple Cobbler

To get a jumpstart on the cooking, zap the apples
in the microwave until the fruit is tender, then top the filling
with a rich buttery crust and bake until golden and flaky.

ACTIVE TIME: 30 MINUTES   **TOTAL TIME:** 1 HOUR 15 MINUTES
MAKES: 12 SERVINGS

COBBLER CRUST

- 1 cup all-purpose flour
- 1½ teaspoons baking powder
- ¼ cup plus 1 tablespoon sugar
- 3 tablespoons cold butter or margarine, cut into ½-inch pieces
- ½ cup plus 1 tablespoon heavy or whipping cream
- ⅛ teaspoon ground cinnamon

APPLE FILLING

- 1 lemon
- 2½ pounds Granny Smith, Golden Delicious, and/or Gala apples (5 to 7 medium), cored, peeled, and cut into ½-inch-thick wedges
- ⅓ cup sugar
- 2 tablespoons cornstarch
- ⅛ teaspoon salt

1 Prepare Cobbler Crust: In medium bowl, combine flour, baking powder, and ¼ cup sugar. With pastry blender or using two knives scissor-fashion, cut in butter until mixture resembles fine crumbs. Add ½ cup cream and stir with fork until dough comes together. Gather dough into ball and place on lightly floured sheet of waxed paper. With floured rolling pin, roll dough into 9-inch round. Slide waxed paper onto cookie sheet and refrigerate dough until ready to use. In cup, mix cinnamon and remaining 1 tablespoon sugar; set aside.

2 Preheat oven to 400°F.

3 Prepare Apple Filling: From lemon, grate ½ teaspoon peel and squeeze 1 tablespoon juice. In large bowl, toss lemon peel and juice with apples, sugar, cornstarch, and salt. Transfer apple mixture to 9½-inch deep-dish glass or ceramic pie plate. Cover with waxed paper and microwave on High until apples are fork-tender, 8 minutes, stirring well halfway through cooking.

4 Immediately, while filling is hot, remove dough round from refrigerator and, with the help of the waxed paper, invert dough over apple mixture. Peel off paper. Cut 4-inch X in center of round; fold back points to make square opening. Brush dough with remaining 1 tablespoon cream; sprinkle with cinnamon-sugar.

5 Bake cobbler until filling is bubbly in center, 35 to 40 minutes. Loosely cover with foil after 25 minutes if top is browning too quickly. Cool cobbler on wire rack.

....

EACH SERVING: ABOUT 195 CALORIES, 2G PROTEIN, 32G CARBOHYDRATE, 8G TOTAL FAT (5G SATURATED), 2G FIBER, 24MG CHOLESTEROL, 110MG SODIUM.

SPICED CHOCOLATE
Bread Pudding

Deep, dark, and oh-so-decadent, this classic dessert pairs
chunks of rich egg bread and semisweet chocolate with
a cinnamon-and-cayenne-pepper-spiked chocolate custard.
Serve drizzled with dulce de leche and scoops
of dulce de leche ice cream for a serious caramel blast.

ACTIVE TIME: 30 MINUTES **TOTAL TIME:** 1 HOUR 30 MINUTES PLUS CHILLING
MAKES: 16 SERVINGS

1   loaf (12 ounces) egg bread, such as challah

3   cups whole milk

1¼ cups sugar

½   teaspoon ground cinnamon

pinch cayenne (ground red) pepper

pinch salt

½   cup heavy or whipping cream

4   ounces unsweetened chocolate, chopped

7   large eggs

6   ounces semisweet chocolate chips or chunks
    (1 cup)

dulce de leche or vanilla ice cream, optional

dulce de leche for drizzling, optional

1 Grease shallow 3-quart baking dish.

2 Cut bread into ¾-inch-thick slices. Toast lightly
until golden brown. Cool completely, then cut
each slice in half diagonally.

3 In 3-quart saucepan, whisk together milk,
sugar, cinnamon, cayenne pepper, salt, and cream
until blended. Heat over medium heat until
bubbles form around edge. Add unsweetened
chocolate and whisk until melted. In large bowl,
whisk eggs until blended. Continue whisking
while adding hot chocolate mixture in slow,
steady stream.

4 In prepared baking dish, decoratively arrange
slices of toast in overlapping layers to cover dish
evenly. Scatter chocolate chips over slices of
toast, then pour chocolate mixture evenly over
all. Cover with plastic wrap. If toast slices are not
coated with chocolate mixture, gently press down
to coat with mixture. Refrigerate at least 1 hour
or up to 1 day.

5 Preheat oven to 350°F. Remove plastic wrap
and bake until knife inserted in center comes out
clean, 45 minutes to 1 hour. Cool on wire rack at
least 15 minutes. Serve with ice cream and drizzle
with dulce de leche, if using.

EACH SERVING: ABOUT 295 CALORIES, 8G PROTEIN,
38G CARBOHYDRATE, 15G TOTAL FAT (8G SATURATED),
2G FIBER, 107MG CHOLESTEROL, 155MG SODIUM.

Index

Note: Page numbers in *italics* indicate photos of recipes located separately from respective recipes.

Photo Credits

FRONT COVER: Cover photography © Con Poulos (front casserole); © Larissa Veronesi/Corbis (front background); © Kate Sears (back)

age footstock: © Leigh Beisch: 96

Depositphotos: © aluha123: 41; © James Baigrie : 14, 115; © bergamont: 66, 81; © Andrey Eremin: 98; © Ispace: 117; © Iakov Kalinin: 22; © Przemyslaw Koch: 22; © Ovydyborets: 119; © photomaru: 34; © spline_x: 16

iStockphoto: © egal: 71; © Christian Fischer: 99 bottom right; © Jamesmcq24: 25; © mariusFM77: 99 bottom left; © mauhorng: 99 center left; © PicturePartners: 95; © SednevaAnna: 99 top; © VadimZakirov: 19

© Francis Janisch: 91

© John Kernick: 108

© Kate Mathis: 24, 28, 40, 44, 67, 78, 106, 109, 110, 118

© Con Poulos: 6, 32, 39, 43, 46, 55, 56, 60, 80, 82, 86, 88, 94, 122

© Kate Sears: 2, 31, 48, 52, 84

Studio D: Philip Friedman: 7; Emily Kate Roemer: 12, 20

Shutterstock: © AS Food studio: 11; © bergamont: 113; © indigolotos: 33; © kaiskynet: 108; © Olga Miltsova: 100; © paulista: 114; © photolinc: 75; © Soulphobia: 57; © Jiang Zhongyan: 99 center left

© Mark Thomas: 26, 36, 59, 64, 70, 73, 102, 105, 116

© Anna Williams: 17, 68, 92

Metric Conversion Charts

The recipes that appear in this cookbook use the standard United States method for measuring liquid and dry or solid ingredients (teaspoons, tablespoons, and cups). The information on this chart is provided to help cooks outside the U.S. successfully use these recipes. All equivalents are approximate.

METRIC EQUIVALENTS FOR DIFFERENT TYPES OF INGREDIENTS

STANDARD CUP *(e.g. flour)*	**FINE POWDER** *(e.g. rice)*	**GRAIN** *(e.g. sugar)*	**GRANULAR** *(e.g. butter)*	**LIQUID SOLIDS** *(e.g. milk)*	**LIQUID**
¾	105 g	113 g	143 g	150 g	180 ml
⅔	93 g	100 g	125 g	133 g	160 ml
½	70 g	75 g	95 g	100 g	120 ml
⅓	47 g	50 g	63 g	67 g	80 ml
¼	35 g	38 g	48 g	50 g	60 ml
⅛	18 g	19 g	24 g	25 g	30 ml

USEFUL EQUIVALENTS FOR LIQUID INGREDIENTS BY VOLUME

¼ tsp	=								1 ml
½ tsp	=								2 ml
1 tsp	=								5 ml
3 tsp	=	1 tbls	=			½ fl oz	=		15 ml
		2 tbls	=	⅛ cup	=	1 fl oz	=		30 ml
		4 tbls	=	¼ cup	=	2 fl oz	=		60 ml
		5⅓ tbls	=	⅓ cup	=	3 fl oz	=		80 ml
		8 tbls	=	½ cup	=	4 fl oz	=		120 ml
		10⅔ tbls	=	⅔ cup	=	5 fl oz	=		160 ml
		12 tbls	=	¾ cup	=	6 fl oz	=		180 ml
		16 tbls	=	1 cup	=	8 fl oz	=		240 ml
		1 pt	=	2 cups	=	16 fl oz	=		480 ml
		1 qt	=	4 cups	=	32 fl oz	=		960 ml
						33 fl oz	=		1000 ml = 1 L

USEFUL EQUIVALENTS FOR DRY INGREDIENTS BY WEIGHT

(To convert ounces to grams, multiply the number of ounces by 30.)

1 oz	=	1⁄16 lb	=	30 g
4 oz	=	¼ lb	=	120 g
8 oz	=	½ lb	=	240 g
12 oz	=	¾ lb	=	360 g
16 oz	=	1 lb	=	480 g

USEFUL EQUIVALENTS FOR COOKING/OVEN TEMPERATURES

	Fahrenheit	*Celsius*	*Gas Mark*
Freeze Water	32° F	0° C	
Room Temperature	68° F	20° C	
Boil Water	212° F	100° C	
Bake	325° F	160° C	3
	350° F	180° C	4
	375° F	190° C	5
	400° F	200° C	6
	425° F	220° C	7
	450° F	230° C	8
Broil			Grill

USEFUL EQUIVALENTS LENGTH

(To convert inches to centimeters, multiply the number of inches by 2.5.)

1 in	=					2.5 cm
6 in	=	½ ft	=			15 cm
12 in	=	1 ft	=			30 cm
36 in	=	3 ft	=	1 yd	=	90 cm
40 in	=					100 cm = 1 m

THE GOOD HOUSEKEEPING
TRIPLE-TEST PROMISE

At *Good Housekeeping*, we want to make sure that every recipe we print works in any oven, with any brand of ingredient, no matter what. That's why, in our test kitchens at the **Good Housekeeping Research Institute**, we go all out: We test each recipe at least three times—and, often, several more times after that.

When a recipe is first developed, one member of our team prepares the dish, and we judge it on these criteria: It must be **delicious**, **family-friendly**, **healthy**, and **easy to make**.

1 The recipe is then tested several more times to fine-tune the flavor and ease of preparation, always by the same team member, using the same equipment.

2 Next, another team member follows the recipe as written, **varying the brands of ingredients** and **kinds of equipment**. Even the types of stoves we use are changed.

3 A third team member repeats the whole process **using yet another set of equipment** and **alternative ingredients**. By the time the recipes appear on these pages, they are guaranteed to work in any kitchen, including yours. **We promise**.